EDITORIAL

This issue concludes the 2023 publishing year, albeit published in 2024 due to the unpredictability of many elements that come together to make a society journal, including managing the time demands of authors and peer reviewers, Editor and production team changes and availability, and at times, the general pace of life in these current times which means over-commitments, juggling multiple hats and roles, and the nature of human life. Thanks to the move to a Society-based publishing model, however, we have been able to publish all the articles in this issue 'online first' as they are finalised, allowing authors to disseminate their findings and experiences as soon as possible. As always, online first articles are available from the Archives and Manuscripts website at publications.archivists.org.au

In this issue, we present three peer-reviewed articles and three reflections on professional practice. Each of the articles interacts with key issues facing the profession today and shares new knowledge and ways of thinking about the challenges, whether they be AI-supported transcription[1] or the use of social media in archival advocacy.[2,3] We also present two articles that challenge the way archivists have historically thought about interacting with communities, both within the records themselves, and those who look to access them. Schilling considers these challenges through description and positionality,[4] while Thieberger et al. consider this through the lens of access and discoverability.[5] These two articles talk to current conversations, both global and within the Australian archival context.

What is common through these six papers is the ongoing commitment to an always emerging archival practice, one where both evidence and experience are regarded as influential, and where there is space for the voices of those with stakes in the work we do to be heard.[1-6] We encourage further submissions to the journal that continue to develop these ideas and give space to the variety of (sometimes competing) voices and stakeholders who are influenced by archival practices.

We would like to take the time in this Editorial to also thank two outgoing Editorial Board members for their commitment to and support of *Archives and Manuscripts* during their tenure on the Board.

Dr Shadrack Katuu (Editorial Board member 2012–2024) is stepping down from his role on the Editorial Board after 12 years, during which he has seen the breadth of work undertaken across the journal. Shadrack joined the Board soon after the transition to the Taylor & Francis publishing model and was involved in the transition to the current open access publishing model. We thank Shadrack for his careful consideration of issues raised by Editors and Council, and especially for his advocacy for academic research taking place outside of traditional research institutions.

Professor Maryanne Dever (Editorial Board member 2019–2023) has had a long standing relationship with *Archives and Manuscripts,* including as Guest Editor of the 2014 special issue *Literary archives, materiality and the digital* (Volume 42 Issue 3). Maryanne was appointed to the Editorial Board in 2019 and has provided guidance and input to three General Editors.

We thank Maryanne for her service to the Board and acknowledge the important role she played in bringing disciplinary knowledge to the Board from outside the information studies discipline.

In 2024, we are looking for new members of the Editorial Board and encourage any interested readers to reach out for more information about what a role on the Board entails.

Angela Schilling and Dr Jessie Lymn
General Editors
journaleditor@archivists.org.au

Notes

1. Kasperowski et al., 'Temporalities and Values in an Epistemic Culture: Citizen Humanities, Local Knowledge, and AI-supported Transcription of Archives', *Archives & Manuscripts*, vol. 51, no. 2, 2023, pp. 3–22.
2. Julie Daly, 'School Archives and the Visibility of Heritage via #throwbackthursday', *Archives & Manuscripts*, vol. 51, no. 2, 2023, pp. 71–76.
3. Laura Sizer, 'Harnessing Social Media to Advocate for the University Archive', *Archives & Manuscripts*, vol. 51, no. 2, 2023, pp. 55–62.
4. Angela Schilling, 'Anti-Racist Archival Description', *Archives & Manuscripts*, vol. 51, no. 2, 2023, pp. 43–54.
5. Nick Thieberger et al., 'The New Protectionism: Risk Aversion and Access to Indigenous Heritage Records', *Archives & Manuscripts*, vol. 51, no. 2, 2023, pp. 23–42.
6. Catherine Banks, 'The Influence of Feminist Archival Theory on State Archival Exhibitions', *Archives & Manuscripts*, vol. 51, no. 2, 2023, pp. 63–70.

ARTICLE

Temporalities and Values in an Epistemic Culture: Citizen Humanities, Local Knowledge, and AI-supported Transcription of Archives

Dick Kasperowski[1]*, Karl-Magnus Johansson[2] and Olof Karsvall[2]

[1]Department of Philosophy, Linguistics and Theory of Science, University of Gothenburg, Sweden; [2]The Swedish National Archives, Stockholm, Sweden

Abstract

An enormous amount of handwritten documents in archives can only be accessed by experts trained in reading older handwriting. Through artificial intelligence (AI)-supported technology, they can now be transcribed and made available for wider audiences. To produce transcriptions an AI needs training and a feasible way is to invite citizens to fulfil such tasks. To understand how an epistemic culture develops in such work, this study conducted interviews with participants on how they associate value, meaning and recognise themselves as active epistemic subjects in relation to the project. Despite that the formation of an epistemic culture are beyond the influence and control of project owners, findings show a strong relation between participants' knowledge of local history, and personal and emotional ties to archival content, for achieving high quality in AI-transcriptions.

Keywords: *Citizen humanities; archives; artificial intelligence; handwritten text recognition; epistemic culture*

The concept of citizen humanities (CH) has in recent years been used to denote the involvement of the public in different aspects of digital humanities and archival research.[1] This aligns with developments within archival studies, where 'participatory archives' has been described as a reconceptualisation of archival practices that questions the inherent power dynamic between archivists and users,[2] changing the archivist's role towards community-based and participatory archiving, as a consequence of the digitalisation and democratising of archives.[3] Initiatives of public involvement include projects on large scale platforms accessible for global audiences, as well as more local arrangements catering for participants with more specific domain expertise.[4] This type of distributed work, beyond the boundaries of professional expertise, can be situated in a general and global context of an 'openness paradigm' encompassing the distribution of tasks in advanced knowledge production known as citizen science (CS) or, as in this paper, CH.

*Corresponding author: Dick Kasperowski, Email: dick.kasperowski@gu.se

Making archives available in digital form is a main task for most archive institutions. For decades, the archives have invested in digitisation, that is, by scanning and photographing physical documents. The Swedish National Archives, for example, holds more than 200 million raster image files of archival documents. In this way, the archives become available instantly, at any time, reducing the need to visit the reading rooms of the institutions. However, documents as raster images, especially handwritten documents, need to be read and interpreted manually.

Developments in artificial intelligence (AI) has changed the conditions for research based on handwritten sources. It also affects the roles of volunteer participants in CH. The enormous number of handwritten documents in the archives, which have long been reserved for experts trained in reading older handwriting, can now be transcribed by machine learning technology, known as handwritten text recognition (HTR). Access to large quantities of machine transcriptions would broaden and deepen research, and notably benefit local heritage and genealogical research. Including HTR and other AI technologies would therefore be an important step to take for the archive institutions. In particular, it would facilitate in-depth full-text searches of archives that are difficult to access and use today.

However, the potential of HTR technology involves a greater challenge: access to high quality training data. The machine needs to learn the language, semantics and handwriting that appear in the various archives. Machine interpretation is thus dependent on transcriptions created by humans manually, as 'ground truth' for training. There are digital platforms such as *Transkribus* that facilitate the work with HTR for non-programmers.[5] But transcribing by hand is time-consuming and requires experience in or knowledge of reading and interpreting older handwriting. Given the enormous amount of preserved historical documents in archives, the need for such transcription processes is far exceeding the available resources at most archival institutions.

A feasible way is to invite citizens to participate with their interest and knowledge of handwritten sources. Galleries, libraries, archives and museums (GLAMs) have a long legacy of promoting participation with the public, and have institutional aims to promote their collections and archives, attracting as wide an audience as possible.[6] This now includes initiatives to invite volunteer participants to either perform tasks that are usually carried out by professional scholars, or work that has never been done by paid employees.[7] Collaborative transcription now appears prominently within the field of participatory archives, as a way to share control of archival content curation with users who often identify themselves as stakeholders in relation to the archives' content.[8] Such work now also encompasses the use of AI, including the training and correcting of handwritten manuscripts for the use of HTR.[9] However, the cultural aspects of such work, particularly the epistemic cultures developing among volunteer contributors are largely unknown. To study the cultural aspects of CH implies to consider the values of participation developing among volunteer participants, values that often are beyond the influence of project owners. Studying epistemic cultures in relation to AI applications, such as HTR, will nuance the focus on optimisation of time and resources often associated with this technology.[10] As such cultural studies offer a new and much needed perspective on the often-occurring presumption that CH participants should be aligned with technology and its protocols for optimisation.

Purpose and research questions

The overarching purpose of this paper is to understand how an epistemic culture in CH develops. More specifically, this leads to the questions of this paper, namely: How do volunteer participants recognise themselves as active epistemic subjects? How do they associate meaning and value to their engagement in transcribing training data and correcting the machine transcription of historical handwritten documents? To answer this, we interviewed volunteer participants engaged in a collaborative AI-supported transcription project initiated by the Swedish National Archives. The project, *The Detective Section*, invited volunteer participants to train an HTR to process 25,000 pages of handwritten text from the 19th century. The findings reported in this paper build upon accounts of volunteer participants' practices and experiences of the project.

Following recent studies of CH and the expected changes in AI-implementations,[11] we apply conceptual resources from studies of epistemic cultures, to understand how volunteer participants associate values and meaning when training an AI. The answers, we believe, will produce a nuanced understanding of why and how tasks are performed by volunteer participants in distributed heritage work involving AI. Eventually such understandings can point to how volunteers value participation. To consider how such practices tie in with the formation of values benefit reflections on the design and scale of future HTR projects. In other words, this study presents a meta-perspective on CH projects combined with AI, which we believe needs to be explored in more detail.

The present paper starts with a description of the studied case, *The Detective Section*, and its relation to CH. Next, the theoretical and methodological framework is outlined, situating our study in motivational studies in CH and CS. We then proceed with our theoretical resources before presenting our empirical results. This is followed by a discussion on the implications of our findings, how meaning and domain expertise in relation to the historical material is important for attaining quality in an HTR process. The paper concludes with how our results transcend standard configurations of volunteer participants in practices of archives and CH.

The Detective Section as a case of handwritten text recognition and citizen humanities
In November 2019, the HTR and CH transcription project *The Detective Section* (Detektiva avdelningen) was initiated at the Swedish National Archives in collaboration with GPS400: Centre for Collaborative Visual Research at the University of Gothenburg.

The archival material in *The Detective Section* included 25,000 pages from the Gothenburg Police department consisting of a series of handwritten police reports 1868–1902, and handwritten copies of received and sent telegraph messages 1865–1903.[12] The information in the material could potentially be of value to many research fields such as historical, cultural and linguistic studies, as well as for amateur research, for example family historians. The material was previously rarely used, however. Since it was not digitised, it had to be read in its original physical form in the reading room; and the catalogue only gave information about what year the records were from, not which persons, places or events that were mentioned. Therefore, to make this series available as fully transcribed text data would radically improve its accessibility and ability to be searched and used. The material was selected both in dialogue with three volunteer participants from a previous participatory project at the National Archives in Gothenburg, as well as with researchers at GPS400. Also, the layout of the handwritten text in the series, with spreads of plain running text, was taken into consideration in the selection since it tends to make the HTR process more efficient.

In the project, the HTR platform *Transkribus* was used to train an HTR model, that is, an algorithm that later on was used for automated transcription of handwritten text.[13] Initially, volunteer participants were invited to join the project and transcribe the training data in an online user interface in *Transkribus*. For this purpose, a mass email was sent on 2 February 2020 to the approximately 500 email addresses used during the last 8 years to inform the public about upcoming lectures at the Gothenburg branch of the Swedish National Archives. Volunteer participants were approached regarding an opportunity to create new ways of conducting research on the local history of Gothenburg. The invitation stated that no previous knowledge was required besides basic computer skills; however, the ability to read handwriting from the years around 1900 would be an asset. The invitation described how the project would radically improve the material's accessibility and ability to be searched and used. It also clearly stated that the final transcriptions would eventually be published as text data on the website of the National Archives, open and free to use for all. Social media platforms were also used to invite volunteer participants with a similar but condensed message. Some of the social media posts went viral, for example, the Twitter invitation reached 7,800 users on the platform.

During an initial 3-month phase, more than 400 spreads with 165,000 words were manually transcribed by five volunteer participants. The transcribed text was then used as training data for an HTR model that was trained to a character error rate of 2.7%. Since the transcribed series in the project was going to be published as text data with as close to 100% correct transcription – as suggested by both the participants and the involved researchers – volunteer participants were again invited to the project, now to proofread and correct the rest of the pages after they were automatically transcribed by the HTR model.

A second invitation mass email was sent on 23 September 2020, specifically asking for participation with proofreading and correcting the automated transcribed documents. The invitation described the success of the initial phase of the project, and also gave examples of the content of the archival material. At the same time, the printed newsletter *Västanbladet* for the local genealogical association, *GöteborgsRegionens släktforskare* [The GothenburgRegion Genealogists] carried a presentation of the project, and the webpage for the Centre for Collaborative Visual Research at the University of Gothenburg described the project and invited volunteer participants to join. Eighteen new volunteer participants joined the project after the second campaign, and all of the previous participants chose to continue in the project.

At the beginning of the project, the project leader wrote a manual in consultation with two of the volunteer participants. The manual was sent to all new participants and included basic instructions on how to perform the tasks as well as recommendations on resources that might be helpful when working in the project, such as databases and encyclopaedias.

When designing the participatory aspects of the project, it was important for the project managers to leverage the experiences gained from previous onsite participatory projects at the National Archives in Gothenburg where participants were invited to interact with analogue material in workshops. Those experiences highlighted the importance of learning and social aspects of such projects, as well as the participants' account of a rewarding feeling of contributing to a greater good.[14] Therefore, starting from 2 months after the first invitation, monthly meetings with volunteer participants were arranged. Because of the restrictions following the coronavirus disease 2019 (COVID-19) pandemic, the meetings had to be digital (via Zoom). The agenda of the meetings was to discuss the work that was done in the project, to share experiences about the difficulties in the assessment of transcriptions and correc-tions, and to share stories contained in the documents and how they relate to or challenge historical knowledge. The volunteer participants were invited to the meetings by the project leader, and the lead researcher at GPS400 was always present. Other researchers that had studied the historical period of the material were invited to some of the meetings to contextualise the work in the project as well as to gain specific knowledge from the volunteer participants. Since the project's archival material reflects the inequalities of Swedish society at the time, experts on gendered crime and social injustice were among the invited scholars. They took part in the discussions adding contextual knowledge about the social structures in which the plaintiffs, defendants and witnesses of the police reports were part. Other invited researchers were scholars of language technology, criminology, and photography.

Theoretical and methodological considerations
Motives for participation in citizen humanities and citizen science

The theoretical framework for this study relies on the concept of epistemic cultures. It was introduced to nuance the distributed knowledge practices in institutional settings of science and research, and to take closer account of how members of such epistemic cultures realise themselves as active epistemic subjects.[15] In this study, these concepts are employed to create a more finely granulated understanding of the motives, values and notions of time among volunteer participants than what is usually offered by studies of participation in CH and CS.

Studies of CH have been concerned with classifying the activities and tasks performed by volunteers, commonly finding that participants are included in assignments of tagging, transcribing, categorising, mapping, georeferencing, contextualising, and translating empirical material.[16] The 'main tasks' in CH projects have been identified as involving refining and collecting data, and in some cases also contributing domain expertise in more collaborative roles of co-creating projects.[17]

The preoccupation with classifying volunteer participants' tasks into different forms of CH has been paired with an interest in what motivates them to engage in projects according to project aims, and the value to institutions of their contributions.[18] In pointing out new directions for 'crowdsourcing in the cultural heritage sector', the increased value for institutions,[19] the possibilities of technological development and understanding volunteer participants' motivation are often suggested as important to explore in the future development of best practices in participatory projects.

Recurrent findings in motivation studies include commitment, learning experiences, personal rewards, interest, purpose, addiction, and good cause.[20] These largely institutional approaches to understanding volunteer participation in the humanities and sciences often find themselves at home in managing and sustaining coordination of distributed work to facilitate productivity, efficiency and timesaving for scientific and cultural heritage institutions. Accordingly, volunteer participants are often invited with tasks that are open to anyone, regardless of training and knowledge,[21] with fine-tuned strategies to uphold motivation,[22] including retention, targeted invitations,[23] and using technology to survey, standardise and speed up processes of data collection and project performance.[24] Recent ethical discussions concerning motivational and retention strategies and the extensive instruction and tutoring of volunteers before being able to contribute to CS and CH projects, have found that they create unethically excessive demands on the time and effort of contributors. Concerns about the increased demands on volunteers to be more engaged, for some bordering on exploitation, will eventually be addressed by participants themselves, who will refrain from involvement and abandon projects.[25]

Institutional approaches often neglect or downplay how volunteer participants more dynamically engage with tasks and the material on hand. Universal frameworks and categories for assessing motivation among volunteer participants to achieve retention have also been suggested. Applying such categories, volunteer participants are configured as inclined to contribute to research, including benevolence (helping people within one's own circle), and self-direction (creating, exploring) as the most important motivators. Categories with a low ranking are self-enhancement motivations of power (gaining recognition and status), achievement (personal success), as well as conformity (adhering to social expectations), personal image or reputation.[26]

We suggest that such approaches and findings largely capture the temporal adaptation, or subordination of volunteer participants to contribute, imposed in speeding up the scientific process, justifying institutional motives, however, largely outside of participants' influence. The cultural perspective employed in this study holds that there are reasons to reconsider such conceptual frameworks concerning participant's motives when understanding participatory cultural heritage work.[27]

A cultural perspective on distribution, tasks and time in citizen humanities
With an increased recognition of the capacity (and necessity) among citizens to be actively involved in research, largely facilitated by the digital development, some studies explore the epistemological ideals and values developing among volunteer participants, as different research fields configure to accommodate 'outsiders' as contributors.[28] The analytical resources offered by the perspective of epistemic cultures lead us to ask different questions regarding the volunteer participants' reasons for participating in CH projects.

The interest in volunteer motivation as a condition for successfully conducting such projects has overshadowed enquiries into what values and knowledge volunteer participants themselves develop as epistemic cultures are formed in such projects. Our conjecture, building on the limited number of studies of epistemic cultures in CS and CH,[29] is that meaning created by volunteer contributors transcends categories of motivation, retention and institutional benefits, as participatory initiatives are considered by museums and archives.[30]

Thus, what do volunteer participants do and how do they find value and meaning in what they do? It has been shown that participants' engagement results in practices and values to create meaning beyond the goals of a project as formulated by owners and initiators. Namely, content to be tagged, transcribed, classified among others, with the help of volunteer participants contain anomalies, surprises, uncertainties and previously unseen or experienced phenomena that spur different types of engagement and practices among volunteer participants.[31] These types of activities have been described in terms of 'epistemic stratification' occurring over time in projects, as actors are endowed with or find temporal epistemic meanings in training an AI.[32]

In recent research on elderly persons engaging in voluntary archival work, results point to the 'good relations' that volunteer participants develop to documents, technologies and the individuals present in historical documents.[33] These findings resonate with what anthropologists and sociologists have called *social time*, offering a conceptual framework of understanding time as 'multiple, heterogeneous and arising from unequal entanglements between various social formations'.[34] This perspective, how time is *made* meaningful and valued as it operates as mediator or intermediary for social collaboration – and coordination, we tentatively suggest, is a resource for understanding the epistemic cultures of CH and distributed cultural heritage work.

The active forming of relationships with time, including to the historical archival material, but also to the future users of the digitised archive, as well as to the task of training the AI for HTR, we postulate, are intimately connected to meaning and values developed in the epistemic cultures of volunteer participants. To be able to transform the historical handwritten documents of *The Detective Section* into text data, volunteer participants trained an AI that was fed with these documents. This transformation relies on the volunteer participants' ability to read sometimes difficult handwritten text. This capacity cannot be separated from their knowledge and interest in the historical time period, as well as the participants' familiarity, knowledge and use of archival and other resources assisting them in their work. The empirical question is what this task will produce in terms of time(s), not only to the material as such, but also in relation to the work requested of, and the time devoted to the project by volunteer participants. How time is made meaningful might also be different between individuals and tasks.[35]

If the assignment to train an HTR model and correct its automated transcriptions is experienced by volunteer participants as a number of well aligned intermediaries making the task smooth and easy, for instance an easy to follow handwriting, an easy to use interface for training the HTR model among others, work might flow, but also be less challenging, and therefore uninteresting. However, if the same tasks are experienced as mediators to overcome, causing the volunteer difficulties, time will be experienced differently, both in relation to the historical material as well as time spent for assignments.

Interviews with volunteer participants

To understand how an epistemic culture develops in distributed AI-supported cultural heritage work, semi-structured interviews with seven volunteer participants in *The Detective Section* were conducted during March–June of 2022. Respondents were approached with the methodological intention of having as heterogeneous a sample as possible of respondents in order to search for commonalities and differences across this diversity and understand the epistemic culture. For this purpose, it was more interesting to examine a few cases in depth and the inclusion of seven respondents was based on methodological considerations that an interval of 6–8 respondents would result in empirical material that would be relatively independent of individual respondents personal or subjective opinions. Generalisations were thus not based on representation, but on comparisons of data from interviews with the aim of identifying similarities and differences between volunteer participants' accounts and arguing for the most likely interpretations of how time was made meaningful and valued. Interviews were coded and analysed by each of the authors independently following a triangulation approach, and each interview was analysed in full.

The aim was to identify themes that arose across interviews, striving for theoretical saturation working back and forth between theory and empirical data to identify shared values and meanings in relation to time.[36] This yielded an identification and preliminary coding of themes that was then compared and grouped together by the authors. This work resulted in four themes, as reported below, of how time was socially made in forming values and meaning by volunteer participants in the project.

Each interview session was conducted in the presence of the interviewing researcher, the project leader, and a volunteer participant. The sessions strived to utilise the interviews in a dialogic way between the individuals present. Conversations revolved around the participants' accounts of their communicative practices as volunteer participants in the project, how they developed and relied on earlier knowledge and experiences as they completed tasks, and how they found meaning and relevance in their involvement.

All interviews were performed with the informed consent of the respondents. All direct quotes from participants used in this paper have been provided following informed consent from respondents and according to the ethical guidelines established by the Swedish Research Council.[37]

All respondents were retired (over 65 years) and the majority had an education well beyond secondary school, in several cases at the university level, including one doctoral exam. The gender distribution was three women and four men. The respondent's contributions to the project ranges from transcribing and/or correcting less than 100 to more than 3,000 documents. Three of the respondents joined the project in the initial phase when the training data was transcribed, and four joined in the second phase. One of the respondents chose to end his engagement because of illness before the project was completed. All of the interviewed volunteer participants had previous knowledge and domain expertise in the use of archives as active genealogists or local historians. Thus, there existed a culture of shared interest and trust among the volunteer participants and the archive. This is exemplified by participation in public lectures and earlier collaborative projects initiated by the National

Archives in Gothenburg, and even in one case by being engaged by them as a lecturer for a public lecture. Some participants had also developed their interest and knowledge of history in university courses, and in authorship of books on local history. This resonates with earlier research on the demographics and education of participants in CS, which found that many participants are highly educated, upper-middle class, middle-aged or older, of higher income, and white.[38] This has also been the case with participants in CHs.[39] The contexts from which many CH projects emanate (genealogy, local history) – having been institutionalised at archives for decades – may prevent more inclusive and equitable participation, however also providing the necessary domain expertise.

Results

In this section, we present our results from interviews with the volunteer participants. This is followed by the four themes that arose across interviews on participants as epistemic subjects; communication and community, working with AI, multiple kinds of relational knowledge, and values in and beyond *The Detective Section*.

Communication and community

Volunteer participants' accounts of being invited into the project point to little or no experience of CS and CH or with training an AI in HTR. The values and meanings associated with participating and devoting time to the project are therefore of a different kind. Instead, it is the unknown, 'exciting' archive and its content that provides the main value. To learn about Gothenburg in the late 1800s and to develop generic knowledge to be applied elsewhere, 'to rummage around in the archive and see what you can find' as one respondent puts it. Or, that it is 'fascinating to follow the fate of humans in a material that brings individuals to life in ways that is not usually found in archives used by genealogists'.

This resonates with the accounts given by respondents on the value of taking part in the project. The particularities of the archive, where people from the past come alive in ways not encountered before, is a shared value emphasised by the volunteer participants, and, but to a lesser extent, the relevance for future research in improving the archive's accessibility and ability to be used and searched. The ground-breaking project of transcribing old handwritten documents with applied AI is not valued to the same extent.

It is apparent that established relations to the archival institution is an important aspect of joining the project. Many participants express having trust in the local branch of the National Archives in Gothenburg. Trust is not about the quality of data, so commonly addressed in CS and CH, but a trust in that the archival institution will facilitate the project in ways that will make taking part interesting and worthwhile. As a respondent with experience from earlier participatory projects at the archives, formulates it:

> There is so much to be found in the Archives, the project helps me to focus on something specific, that I did not know I was interested in. You get that for free, you can contribute, and you learn beyond that.

This form of trust, making things interesting and meaningful, is often grounded in former experiences of taking part in events and activities offered by the National Archives in Gothenburg. These include the established traditions of lectures and workshops offered since 2013. All respondents point to the newsletters as having been the place they were invited into the project rather than the invitations posted on social media, which virally reached many more potential volunteer participants.

The project leader of *The Detective Section* held regular Zoom-meetups with the participants, and invited lecturers to some of the meetings. For ethical and integrity reasons, email addresses were not shared between participants, and no other means of communication between participants, such as social media, was offered. Where volunteer participants required tutoring or encountered problems, the project leader was approached through email. Volunteer participants did not regard the on-line Zoom meetings as specifically discussing the transcription process, and the training of the HTR model. However, they referred to these meetings as opportunities to further develop their historical knowledge and interests. through lectures by invited researchers.

The Zoom meet-ups have been very nice. I felt really privileged to meet the invited researchers. That added value to the project.

Zoom meetings were described by respondents as 'always interesting', but not there for a dialogue on the specifics of AI-supported transcription. However, they created a feeling of belonging to a collective with a shared interest among volunteer participants, and of being needed and appreciated by the project leader and invited lecturers. Some respondents missed the opportunities of in-person meetings to communicate with other volunteer participants on the content of the archives and the local history of Gothenburg in the late 1800s. Physical meetings could have provided better conditions for such discussions, some respondents tentatively suggest, however the 'pandemic put a stop' to such initiatives.

Although the volunteer participants had earlier experience and domain expertise in genealogy and local history, taking part in the project did not inspire or facilitate communication in such networks on their behalf. One exception is a participant who presented the project in a bulletin for a genealogical society. However, several of the interviewed participants shared details of the content of the historical police reports with close friends and family via email and social media but mostly in personal encounters, which evoked 'interest and fascination'.

I've been talking to all of my friends about this project. I'm saying 'I'm doing something really fun', making everyone envious now during Covid.

Me and my friends often take walks in the city. For many places that we pass I can relate to cases and events in the police reports, and I'm always talking about that. It's almost like I'm doing guided city walks for my friends.

Despite this, no one has been able to recruit volunteer participants into the project from these personal networks. The main communication on the tasks distributed within the project, that is, correcting automated transcriptions, has taken place on an individual level between the project leader and volunteer participants.

I have sent texts that I do not understand to [the project leader] and then we have read [them] together.

One respondent wished for possibilities to communicate directly with developers at *Transkribus*. However, this is a rare exception, as Zoom meetings, but interactions with friends and family about the close encounters with individuals in the archives of *The Detective Section*, have been the main content shared with actors outside the project. Thus, the social making of time in the community of volunteer participants is largely defined by the fascination with the past, in a highly local or personal context.

Working with HTR

Although initially invited to transcribe handwritten text as training data for an HTR model, the overwhelmingly majority of time that the volunteer participants spent in the project was working with correcting text that the model had automatically transcribed.

In the interviews, participants closely describe their approach to accomplishing the task of correcting transcriptions as one of switching between levels. This is explained as a move back and forth between individual signs or letters, and the meaning of the text and the context. How this switching between levels occurs is dependent on the complexity of what the HTR model has transcribed:

> First you read to simply correct the straightforward mistakes of form and pattern recognition. The AI might have mistaken a letter because of an unusual form that can be assigned to a particular police officer's handwriting. But when the obvious mistakes are corrected, you have to go to the level of meaning and context, unless you are presented with something very complicated from the start, then you must go for the level of meaning right from the start, to grasp the correct reading of individual letters that the AI has made mistakes about. Then you need the meaning of the text, and maybe the context also.

The usual approach for correcting transcriptions is, however, not to start at the level of meaning as 'the handwriting is so messy'. Participants express the need to start with the single letters that the HTR model has failed to recognise, as it is not yet sufficiently sensitive to the different styles of handwriting in the archive. Moving up to the level of meaning and context is useful at the second stage of correcting. This is when you benefit from understanding the 'flow of the text'.

The repetitive nature of correcting transcriptions is brought up by several respondents. It is the difficult cases, the correct interpretation of vague styles of handwriting to train the HTR model, understanding meaning and text in relation to image and pattern, that challenges participants. However, the difficulties, for some impossibilities, of producing a flawless, perfect, correction is also recognised. Participants have developed slightly different methods of achieving accuracy, repeatedly switching between levels, sometimes letting the first corrected version of a text rest for weeks before returning to it:

> It is very hard to be completely perfect. At the first glance, I see 6–8 errors per page. Then I switch to the level of meaning and it is at this instance that I understand the text for the first time. Earlier, it was just word for word to get the correction of the transcription right, not on the level of meaning. There is no flow when you concentrate on the first correction. [...] When I switch to the level of meaning I find even more mistakes. Then I let the text rest for about two weeks before returning to it, controlling it letter by letter, finding at least one to two additional mistakes per page.

> It is about being true to forms of letters, not trying to write up some content. The AI recognises images and patterns, it is not about content and meaning. That is something for us humans.

This volunteer participant clearly states that reading on the level of meaning and the use of local historical knowledge is a means to attain the non-contextual pattern recognition ability of a well-trained HTR model. To be able to produce an HTR model that can be applied to different text material from the time period and travel extensively between archives, meaning and local context is necessary in producing a high quality HTR model.

The more complicated the handwriting, and the correction needed for the mistakes made by the HTR model, the more you benefit from knowledge about the local historical context.

Usually, the content of reports filed in the archive are not regarded as particularly complicated to read, but the level of difficulty varies as it is connected to the complexity of the handwriting. This is directly related to which scribe the writing can be assigned to, as his style of handwriting would entail recurrent 'unusual forms' of letters, misspellings, word sequences and general style and use of language. Some of the handwriting was regarded by participants and the project leader as the most difficult in the material. In such cases, the automated transcriptions could actually 'train' the participant, hence working with AI is a process of training and being trained:

> Some pages were very difficult to transcribe. To guide me, I checked the automated transcription done by the AI [...] so, you could say that I was also trained by the AI.

Furthermore, the names of streets and geographical locations, the stolen goods, the modus operandi of the crime etc., would provide context from which corrections to the transcripts could be derived. Even though participants had no experience in the type of distributed work that involves training an HTR model on complicated handwritten text, they all had expertise, and in some cases advanced expertise in reading historical handwriting. The added task of working with HTR did not therefore create any great difficulties, except for some very difficult personal styles of handwriting and linguistic conventions, but then the AI could actually be a resource, as its original translations could be checked for clues in how to correct the translations. However, the mistakes by the HTR model could also be a source of irritation:

> Punctuation makes me insane! Particularly when the AI has added it when it is not there in the original text.

The introductory manual was regarded as informative on HTR, but, relying on their domain expertise in deciphering handwritten text, a more common approach among participants was to directly try out the *Transkribus* interface in correcting the automated transcriptions. The value of the manual was instead associated with it being a guide to external resources for completing the task:

> I used several of the digital resources mentioned in the manual, such as historical census data, The Swedish Academy Dictionary and The Swedish State Calendar.

Individual participants also extensively used already cultivated external resources, ranging from Google, to databases at the National Library of Sweden, historical dictionaries, shipping lists, digitised newspapers, place name registers, Wikipedia, catechetical registers in church records etc. The familiarity with archival research and the domain expertise in genealogy and local history was hereby evident among participants.

Additional resources were also developed by individual participants and shared through the project leader and in Zoom meetings as the project progressed. This included a glossary of different textiles, as the most reported crime was the theft of clothes and other textiles, and a list of mortgage offices in Gothenburg. The result of this participants' initiative was an extensive description of over 100 historical terms that was then included in the manual as a resource for all.

Multiple kinds of relational knowledge

Despite their familiarity with archival research, and domain expertise in areas such as the local history of Gothenburg or in reading handwritten historical documents, participants are often eager to point out a cognitive or social distance to 'proper' research, and identify as amateurs who appreciate the opportunity to be of use and provide assistance. In this context, many respondents also point out that their contribution is modest, and that the time spent on tasks in the project is not extensive, as 'I stop before I get bored'.

Increased and detailed knowledge about the local history, however, is a recurrent theme in the respondents' accounts of the value of participating in the project. One participant has, after enrolling in the project, started to re-read her vast collection of historical Gothenburgiana, 'with fresh eyes'. Participants encounter and learn about the fate of individuals, and the places and circumstances of petty crimes in the archives of *The Detective Section*, which they describe as 'exciting' and not encountered before. They also point to the wealth of documentation in the archive that extends beyond the reports on criminal activities and concerns the wider social and technological developments during the time period. Respondents frequently testify to cultivating a 'closeness' to the individuals present in the historical material.

> When you get close to the people you read about in the material, you sometimes feel that you *know* specific bicycle thieves.

Individual scribes of the Police administration are recognised through their use of language and handwriting. In some cases, the personality of the scribe is constructed from the handwriting:

> Someone, in the beginning I called him 'The Klutz', starts to write and then revise over and over again. Writing in between the lines with smaller and smaller letters. Impossible to decipher. It was like as if he was very uncertain about how to communicate and express himself, he seemed to lack self-confidence. His first draft usually was good, but then he always succumbed to extensive revisions. Such a conflict of ambition and ability.

Multiple kinds of relations to the historic material are made by volunteer participants. For yet another participant, with a professional background as a lawyer and judge in the 1970s, closeness is manifested in the familiarity with the language used in police reports: 'I have no difficulties in understanding the content of the material'. Instead, it is the difficult handwriting and era-specific grammatical conventions that constitute an historical challenge and motivate this participant: 'Legal text from the 1890s is not difficult to understand, but what is really meaningful and motivating is to have a difficult handwriting to decipher'.

The challenges of learning to interpret difficult handwriting, and the generic proficiency in this required for genealogical studies in general, is shared by participants: 'You become better in interpreting and reading old handwritten text'. The development of this skill is also connected to having insights into how AI is used to digitise historical archives. It is 'interesting to see how the AI is developing as I help to train it'. The accounts of how knowledge develops during the task of transcribing text and correcting the transcriptions of the HTR model often revolves around how participants develop hermeneutical skills to interpret and understand old handwritten text – and in some instances also the author behind the text.

The language used in the police reports is of central concern to the participants, who refer to the reports as narratives about individuals that you come close to in ways that are rare in historical documents: 'You get to know the individuals'. Geographical references, street names and buildings are spaces adding a closeness in time to the historical period, 'street names are the same as today, it feels very modern'. To have a connection to 'real' people in a transformative period in Swedish history, 'the social and technological development of the period' is experienced as very rare and of a high value. The historical material, through its focus on the fate of individual lives, brings the history alive and closer to participants. In particular, the social inequalities displayed in the material seem to create empathy: 'The insights I got from the material was so interesting, yet so very tragic and sad'.

Some respondents describe an emotional connection to the subjects in the police reports, or, as described in another section above, to scribes identified from their specific handwriting. Recent discussions in archival studies highlight and theorise such connections. People working with archives form emotional relationships with individuals 'from' the archives, sometimes including very sensitive and personal details. Most archival records, and not least the police reports, have an 'intrinsic humanity'.[40]

It is through 'facts' (street names, geographical locations, legal jargon etc.), intertwined with the interpretation and emotions associated with the fate of individuals –'why are they committing these crimes'– that participants return to in explaining how they develop knowledge and meaning in the project. The joining of facts and emotions, text and context in the making of time, actually makes interpretation of difficult handwriting, and the training of the HTR model, possible. In fact, the more you develop your knowledge about the local history of both police officers and their individual use of language and handwriting as well as the delinquents' deeds and fates, the better you can fulfil the task of training the HTR model.

Values in and beyond The Detective Section

For volunteer participants, taking part in *The Detective Section* has enabled them to get access to an historical archive they have not before considered or even known about. As a result, they have been introduced to and developed new knowledge of the local history of Gothenburg:

> I have learned so much about the time period from this project.

> Learning was an important part of expectation when I joined this project ... now I have learned so much and found new interest.

Some participants also point to the understanding they have gained in the role of AI and HTR, but foremost, the high value associated with the opportunity to follow individual cases, 'people' that come alive in an 'exciting archive', and thereby to deepen their understanding of the local history of Gothenburg. Being given the opportunity to understand the workings of an historical public authority and its contemporary context is highly valued by participants. This active forming of 'good relations' to the material and individuals in the historical archive is closely connected to meaning and value among volunteer participants.[41] Some considered this the sole value of taking part:

> The project has created value for me in creating access to the archive and through the tasks of developing the AI. I don't think so much about the wider significance of the work that we have put in.

Others regard their participation as 'making a difference' for the future use of the archive:

> Many will, once the archive is digitised, be able to search through the archive, using names, places, time. There is a need, future genealogists will be able to find their relatives and what they were up to. You are contributing to a common good.

Everyone who has any experience of archive use has also experienced the difficulty of access. What has been done in this project might be important for future generations that would be interested in increased access and searchability of archives. It will be so much easier to have a digitised archive to search and it will be easier for those who do not have the knowledge background, but would like to develop it.

For some, their engagement has spurred further, more specific historical interest in the role of law enforcement. The archive of *The Detective Section* depicts petty crime, mostly thefts, and volunteer participants now ask where reports on other, more serious aspects of law enforcement can be found and investigated. This provides an opportunity to initiate and develop new projects, building on and developing the knowledge on local history that has been gained from taking part in *The Detective Section*. In one case, a volunteer participant initiated their own parallel project out of curiosity about the subjects described in the police reports and started researching them in other archives to find their date of birth, date of death, spouses, children, and even photos of them. The result was a database with information about hundreds of historical individuals, which the volunteer participant then sent to the project leader for distribution to students and others that might find it useful. This parallel project, as well as the glossary list of textiles described earlier, are examples of how the epistemic culture of the project supported participants to initiate and do things beside the main protocol of training an AI.

One respondent is also asking about the possibility of assuming roles in projects beyond correcting automated transcriptions, and whether volunteer participants could be given the opportunity to choose which archives should undergo digitalisation. This also includes the question of how distributed cultural heritage work will be initiated and governed in the future. What roles would archives play in this? What would be the ethical concerns? However, the majority of respondents point to the value of participation *per se*, trusting the archives to facilitate and develop their domain expertise and interests. Here, the participants express an attitude of not questioning their position in the participatory structure, as long as other values in the epistemic culture can be nurtured.

In addition to developing the participants' historical knowledge, and improving their ability to read difficult handwriting while training and developing an HTR model, the value of taking part in the project thus also extends to expectations on the part of the participants of more active participation and access to archives in the future. This connects to the perception among participants of the value of developing AI in making archives accessible to a larger general public and to improve the conditions for future research. Free accessibility to digital archives is emphasised: 'It is important that money is not made from our work. It is a matter of trust'.

Sweden has a long tradition of open access to information in archives, with the world's oldest regulation regarding public access to official records dating back to 1766. Personal and other kinds of sensitive information can be subjected to secrecy, but, not for longer than 70 years. Also, the Swedish implementation of General Data Protection Regulation (GDPR) can limit the distribution of information, but only regarding persons still alive. The material of the project dates from 1865 to 1903, and thus are juridically granted open access.

However, in addition to the juridical aspects, the notion of access is far from neutral.[42] As most of the volunteer participants are part of the family history-community in Sweden, they can be seen as stakeholders in the transcription process that leads to open access. One of the interviewed participants exemplifies this clearly when telling that her husband's family was living in the poorest area of Gothenburg at the time. Another interviewee revealed that his great-great-grandfather was a police officer at the time, but lost his position because of alcohol consumption at work. For both the public access to such information, was a most important reason to even join the project and spend time in it.

Discussion

The respondents stated that local knowledge is a key aspect of understanding this remediation of data. This aligns with studies that challenges whether being digital is being independent from local constraints. Such a perspective suggest that data are entangled within a knowledge system and inscribed in a place, and that all knowledge systems are rooted in practices and politics related to their time and space – that all data are local.[43] This study also acknowledges that these are important aspects to consider in regards to how data quality is attained in distributed cultural heritage work. A large number of studies have been devoted to the question of how to engage volunteer participants in scientific work without compromising the collection and classification of data,[44] and how to facilitate the development of skills that ensure the quality of data. Usually these discussions lead to recommendations for having a low cognitive threshold for volunteer participants, thereby minimising the need for instruction and learning. However, projects such as our *The Detective Section* also rely on the existing domain expertise of the volunteers.[45]

Danielsen et al. (2005) argue that 'locally-based methods are generally more vulnerable than professional techniques to various sources of bias', suggesting 'thorough training' as a solution.[46] However, extensive training is expensive, time consuming and demands infrastructural solutions, therefore the answer often found, according to Danielsen, is to create stable protocols that put volunteer contributors on par with professionals with regard to their tasks. If such stabilisation cannot be attained, professionals, researchers or other actors, including machines (like *Transkribus*) relying on advanced knowledge, will remain sceptical about the results.[47] Volunteer participants before autumn 2020 had created training data for an HTR-model that reached 97.3% certainty in transcribing the handwritten text. As the project was striving for even higher certainty in the HTR transcription ability, it needed more help. The interviews show that the volunteer participants are aware that higher certainty is attained through more persistent work rooted in local knowledge of history and interests in the specific source material. This is despite the fact that AI (HTR) often makes invisible what knowledge and relation to the material is needed to produce an even higher data quality.[48]

Such nuances of delegated work are largely missing in discussions of the significance of domain expertise in distributed cultural heritage work for creating high quality in HTR. It is not only the level of standardisation in the interface or participatory protocol that determines the data quality achieved by volunteer contributors.[49] The focus of our study – how volunteer participants realise themselves as active epistemic subjects – yields that the development of relations to the historical archive illustrates how quality in HTR is improved in ways not usually part of discussions in CH.

Taking account of our empirical results, we have to consider both the spatial aspects of the term 'local' but also its temporal aspects. These temporal features include the relations formed not only with a technological interface or protocol but also with the conditions in which those data have been manifested, that is, close and personal relationships with a local archive. Here respondent accounts of meaning are associated with the stories of individual fates in the historical material. This is important for arriving at a more finely granulated understanding of the training of an AI. It is also clear that the local knowledge systems of connected resources such as databases, other archive series, and encyclopaedias are important when performing such tasks. These circumstances are partly supported by findings in both large globally distributed as well as in smaller scale local participatory projects. Volunteer participants will engage dynamically with the material at hand, often beyond the tasks they have been invited to perform, and will create new resources to share among members.[50] However, this study clearly connects such dynamic relations (of time and local circumstances) to the quality of the work asked for – training an HTR model. Furthermore, emotional relations seem to be important for both creating meaning as well as for the quality of training of the HTR. Emotions are not usually considered important or relevant to include in research, in fact the opposite: they should be avoided or controlled so as not to create bias, thereby contrasting the usual standards for the rigours of knowledge creation.[51] In fact, Danielsen et al. associate 'locally-based' methods with bias.[52]

On the other hand, the accounts from the volunteer contributors in this study show that relations, emotions and empathy together with local historical knowledge are at the core of creating an HTR with high accuracy. Inviting participants with domain expertise in the local history to work together with local historical archives is important for the quality of HTR. The participants' interview responses point to locally 'rooted' projects, in the sense of archival material and voluntary participants with domain expertise, as well as trusted relationships to archival institutions, being favourable. For distributed projects in science and the humanities, open archives and data repositories tend to invite individuals to facilitate efficiency and speed in science and research. In this way, they tend to follow dominant narratives of acceleration so often reiterated in the justification of open science and open data, namely increased production of knowledge and research. However, as the data from the (albeit a limited amount of) in-depth interviews in this study show, the design of projects in archival HTR benefit from a perspective sensitive of time as not exclusively influenced or defined by dominant narratives that describe time as uniform, external to participants and in a state of continuous acceleration.[53] The results align with recent reconceptualisations within archival studies, where indigenous scholars question the pace of archival work and suggest that slowing down creates possibilities to emphasise how such epistemological processes are entangled with a series of relationships.[54] Such 'slow archives' work makes time for people-centred and reflective approaches, and, as shown in this study, this is to the benefit of data quality. These are aspects of an epistemic culture that should be considered in relation to participants' local domain expertise and interests in creating improved digital access to archives.

Conclusion

The purpose of this paper has been to understand how an epistemic culture develops in a distributed CH-project, namely training an AI in HTR. To this end, interviews were conducted with volunteer participants to gain insights into how participants associate value and meaning in relation to the historical material as they transcribe training data and correct automated transcriptions of handwritten documents.

The central finding in this study is the relationship between the volunteer participants' knowledge of local history and their achievement of high quality when correcting the automated transcriptions of the archived material prepared by the HTR model. A recurrent narrative is the participants' accounts of specific local historical knowledge as an important asset for the quality of the correction of transcriptions. The more you develop your knowledge about the local history, in fact establish a personal and emotional relationship to the police officers and scribes, as well as delinquents, the better you can accomplish the task of training the HTR model. The participants' accounts of their engagement with the project show that values and meaning are formed in developing a relationship to the historical material.

Rather than considering optimisation from a technical perspective, we have investigated it in relation to the epistemic culture and the way volunteer participants realise themselves as active epistemic subjects, foremost how they associate meaning and value to their engagement. This perspective has also been recognised in recent studies on participatory AI, acknowledging that communities and citizens beyond technical designers have knowledge and interests that would benefit such projects.[55] The specific tasks at hand, of transcribing training data and correcting automated transcriptions, are not referred to by respondents as the main reason or the meaning of engaging in the project. Volunteer participants are curious about AI and HTR, but it is the relationships formed, bridging time, and the possibilities of discoveries in the archival material that are of central value for the respondents. However, the participants emphasise the importance of generally increased digital access to archives, and in that sense, HTR is a key factor.

These results transcend the categorisations often associated with volunteer participants' motives for taking part in CH. In this case, *The Detective Section,* volunteers have been invited with the task of working with AI in transcribing historical material. Thus, the project is contributive in this respect. It is also collaborative in refining data and creating resources for volunteer participants and furthermore develops domain expertise among them. To be a volunteer participant in *The Detective Section* is to create meaning as you engage and situate yourself in, but also beyond, such categorisations.

Acknowledgments

We would like to thank volunteer participants for generously offering their time and knowledge in interviews. All direct quotes from participants used in this paper have been done so with informed consent. The research was undertaken in collaboration between the Swedish National Archives and The University of Gothenburg.

Conflicting interest and funding

The author(s) declare no potential conflicts of interest with respect to the research, authorship, and/or publication of this article. Information withheld pending peer review. This research was supported by a grant from The Swedish National Heritage Board, RAÄ-2021-2704, *Transcription node Sweden – machine learning and citizen science combined*. PI: Olof Karsvall.

Author biographical notes

Dick Kasperowski
Professor of Theory of Science at the University of Gothenburg. His interests include citizen science, governance of science, participatory and activist practices in science and the humanities and open collaborative projects in scientific work. The analytical focus of his research concerns how new technologies configure relations and the development of epistemic cultures between actors claiming different experiences and knowledge.

Karl-Magnus Johansson
Senior archivist at the Swedish National Archives. In practice and theory, his main interests are understanding engagement in and use of archives, as well as the intersection between media theory, contemporary art and archives.

Olof Karsvall
Research manager at the Swedish National Archives and PhD in Agrarian History. He has been working in several research projects concerning digitalisation, digital methods and research data at the National Archives.

Notes

1. Joni Adamson, 'Gathering the Desert in an Urban Lab: Designing the Citizen Humanities', in Joni Adamson and Michael Davis (eds.), Humanities for the Environment: Integrating Knowledge, Forging New Constellations of Practice, Routledge, London, 2018, pp. 106–19.
2. Edward Benoit III and Alexandra Eveleigh, 'Defining and Framing Participatory Archives in Archival Science', in Edward Benoit III and Alexandra Eveleigh (eds.), Participatory Archives: Theory and Practice, Facet, London, 2019, pp. 1–7.
3. Terry Cook, 'Evidence, Memory, Identity, and Community: Four Shifting Archival Paradigms', Archival Science, vol. 13, 2013, pp. 113–16; Craig Gauld, 'Democratising or Privileging: The Democratisation of Knowledge and the Role of the Archivist', Archival Science, vol. 17, 2017, p. 227.
4. Dick Kasperowski and Thomas Hillman, 'The Epistemic Culture in an Online Citizen Science Project: Programs, Antiprograms and Epistemic Subjects', Social Studies of Science, vol. 48, no. 4, 2018, pp. 567–68.
5. https://readcoop.eu/transkribus/
6. Compare with Melissa Terras, 'Crowdsourcing in the Digital Humanities', in Susan Schreibman, Ray Siemens and John Unsworth (eds.), *A New Companion to Digital Humanities*, John Wiley & Sons, Chichester, 2016, p. 6.
7. Amy Clothworthy, 'The Experience of the Citizen Scientist', Edited interview with Amy Clotworthy, Danish National Archives, 2019b, available at https://training.parthenos-project.eu/wp-content/uploads/2019/05/Amy-Clotworthy-Interview-on-the-Citizen-Scientist-experience-April-2019.pdf; Tim Causer, Kris Grint, Anna-Maria Sichani and Melissa Terras, '"Making Such Bargain": Transcribe Bentham and the Quality and Cost-Effectiveness of Crowdsourced Transcription', Digital Scholarship in the Humanities, vol. 33, no. 3, September 2018, pp. 467–487. see Danish National Archives' crowdsourcing portal https://cs.rigsarkivet.dk.
8. Sumayya Ahmed, 'Engaging Curation: A Look at the Literature on Participatory Archival Transcription', in Edward Benoit III and Alexandra Eveleigh (eds.), Participatory Archives: Theory and Practice, Facet, London, 2019.
9. Compare with Melissa Terras, 'Inviting AI into the Archives: The Reception of Handwritten Recognition Technology into Historical Manuscript Transcription', in Lise Jaillant (ed.), Archives, Access and Artificial Intelligence: Working with Born-Digital and Digitized Archival Collections, Bielefeld University Press, Bielefeld, 2022, p. 188.
10. Compare with Gregory Rolan, et al., 'More Human than Human? Artificial Intelligence in the Archive', Archives and Manuscripts, vol. 47, no. 2, 2019, p. 186.
11. Compare with Jonathon Hutchinson, 'Digital Intermediation: Unseen Infrastructures for Cultural Production', New Media & Society, August 2021.
12. https://riksarkivet.se/psidata/goteborgs-poliskammare
13. For a thorough presentation of Transkribus and its impact on research, see Guenter Muehlberger et al., 'Transforming Scholarship in the Archives through Handwritten Text Recognition: Transkribus as a Case Study', Journal of Documentation, vol. 75, no. 5, September 2019, pp. 954–976.
14. Karl-Magnus Johansson, 'Hungerkravallerna 1917: deltagande i fokus i arbetet med ny utställning i Göteborg', Nordisk Arkivnyt, no. 2, 2017; Karl-Magnus Johansson, 'Medskapande, design och film: ny arkivutställning i Göteborg', Nordisk Arkivnyt, no. 1, 2019.
15. Karin Knorr-Cetina, 'Culture in Global Knowledge Societies: Knowledge Cultures and Epistemic Cultures', Interdisciplinary Science Reviews, vol. 32, no. 4, 2007, pp. 361–375; Karin Knorr-Cetina, Epistemic Cultures: How the Sciences Make Knowledge, Harvard University Press, Cambridge, MA, 1999.
16. Stuart Edale Dunn and Mark Charles Hedges, 'From the Wisdom of Crowds to Going Viral: The Creation and Transmission of Knowledge in the Citizen Humanities', in Christothea Herodotou, Mike Sharples and Eileen Scanlon (eds.), *Citizen Inquiry: Synthesising Science and Inquiry Learning*, Routledge, London, 2017; Dick Kasperowski, Christopher Kullenberg and Frauke Rohden, 'The Participatory Epistemic Cultures of Citizen Humanities: Bildung and Epistemic Subjects', in Palmyre Pierroux, Per Hetland and Line Esborg (eds.), A History of Participation in Museums and Archives: Traversing Citizen Science and Citizen Humanities, Routledge, London, 2020.

17. Kasperowski et al., p. 238; Nina Simon, The Participatory Museum, Museum 2.0, Santa Cruz, 2010.
18. Terras, p. 8; Lesley Parilla and Meghan Ferriter, 'Social Media and Crowdsourced Transcription of Historical Materials at the Smithsonians Institution: Methods for Strenghtening Community Engagement and Its Tie to Transcription Output', The American Archivist, vol. 79, no 2, 2016, pp. 438–460.
19. Ibid, p. 13.
20. Ibid, pp. 13–14; Rose Holley, 'Crowdsourcing: How and Why Should Libraries Do It?', *D-Lib Magazine*, vol. 16, no. 3–4, March 2010, p 1–21.
21. Kasperowski et al., p. 237.
22. Anne Land-Zandstra, Gaia Agnello and Yaşar Selman Gültekin, 'Participants in Citizen Science', in Katrin Vohland, et al. (eds.), *The* Science of Citizen Science, Springer, Cham, 2021, p. 247 ff.
23. Barbara Heinisch, et al., "Citizen Humanities", in Katrin Vohland et al. (eds.), The Science of Citizen Science, Springer, Cham, 2021, pp. 97–118.
24. Bálint Balázs et al., 'Data Quality in Citizen Science', in Katrin Vohland et al. (eds.), The Science of Citizen Science, Springer, Cham, 2021, p. 152.
25. Loreta Tauginienė et al., 'Ethical Challenges and Dynamic Informed Consent', in Katrin Vohland et al. (eds.), The Science of Citizen Science, Springer, Cham, 2021, p. 408; Dick Kasperowski, Niclas Hagen and Frauke Rohden, 'Ethical Boundary Work in Citizen Science: Themes of Insufficiency', *Nordic Journal of Science and Technology Studies*, vol. 10, no. 1, 2021, p. 18.
26. Land-Zandstra et al., p. 249.
27. Compare with Amy Clotworthy, 'Engaging the Human in Digital-Humanities Projects: How Participating in Crowdsourcing Projects Impacts Quality of Life among Volunteers at the Danish National Archives', Paper presented at 4th Digital Humanities in the Nordic Countries, Copenhagen, Denmark, 2019a; Kasperowski and Hillman, 2018; Kasperowski et al., 2020.
28. Knorr-Cetina, p. 367; Kasperowski et al., 2020.
29. Ponti, M., Kasperowski, D. & Gander, A.J. Narratives of epistemic agency in citizen science classification projects: ideals of science and roles of citizens. AI & Soc (2022). https://doi.org/10.1007/s00146-022-01428-9
30. See Mia Ridge et al., *The Collective Wisdom Handbook: Perspectives on Crowdsourcing in Cultural Heritage*, community review version (1st ed.), British Library Publications, London, UK, 2021.
31. Kasperowski and Hillman, 2018, p 582. Full reference for Latour is missing. Should be Bruno Latour Reassembling the social: an introduction to actor-network-theory. Oxford New York: Oxford, University Press, p. 5.
32. Compare with Ponti et al., 2022, p. 13.
33. Clotworthy 2019b, pp. 1–4.
34. Larissa Pschetz and Michelle Bastian, 'Temporal Design: Rethinking time in design', *Design Studies*, vol 56, 2018, pp. 169–184, 172.
35. Latour Reassembling the social: an introduction to actor-network-theory. Oxford New York: Oxford, University Press, p. 5.
36. See Svend Brinkmann and Steinar Kvale, *InterViews: Learning the Craft of Qualitative Research Interviewing*, 3rd ed., Sage Publications, Los Angeles, CA, 2015; Favourate Y. Sebele-Mpofu, 'Saturation Controversy in Qualitative Research: Complexities and Underlying Assumptions: A Literature Review', *Cogent Social Sciences*, vol. 6, no. 1, 2020, 1838706.
37. Swedish Research Council Expert Group on Ethics, *Good Research Practice*, Swedish Research Council, Stockholm, Sweden, 2017.
38. Karen Purcell, Cecilia Garibay and Janis L. Dickinson, 'A Gateway to Science for All: Celebrate Urban Birds', in Janis L. Dickinson and Rick Bonney (eds.), *Citizen Science: Public Participation in Environmental Research*, Cornell University Press, Ithaca, NY, 2012; Rajul Pandya and Kenne Ann Dibner (eds.), *Learning through Citizen Science: Enhancing Opportunities by Design*, The National Academies Press, Washington, DC, 2018; B. Troy Frensley et al., 'Bridging the Benefits of Online and Community Supported Citizen Science: A Case Study on Motivation and Retention with Conservation-Oriented Volunteers', *Citizen Science: Theory and Practice*, vol. 2, no. 1, 2017, 1–14; Elli J. Theobald et al., 'Global Change and Local Solutions: Tapping the Unrealized Potential of Citizen Science for Biodiversity Research', *Biological Conservation*, vol. 181, 2015, pp. 236–44; Hillary K. Burgess et al., 'The Science of Citizen Science: Exploring Barriers to Use as a Primary Research Tool', *Biological Conservation*, vol. 208, 2017, pp. 113–120; Dale R. Wright et al., "Understanding the Motivations and Satisfactions of Volunteers to Improve the Effectiveness of Citizen Science Programs", *Society & Natural Resources*, vol. 28, no. 9, 2015, pp. 1013–29; Mari Jönsson et al., 'Long-Term Trends in Age and Gender Participation in an Online Biodiversity Citizen Science Project', accepted for Ambio, 2023.

39. Chiara Bonacchi et al., "Participation in Heritage Crowdsourcing", Museum Management and Curatorship, vol. 34, no. 2, 2019, pp. 166–82.
40. Jennifer Douglas, et al., '"These Are Not Just Pieces of Paper": Acknowledging Grief and Other Emotions in Pursuit of Person-Centered Archives', Archives & Manuscripts vol. 50, no. 1, 2022, pp. 5–29.
41. Compare with Clotworthy, 2019a and Clothworthy, 2019b.
42. Agostinho, Daniela, 'Archival Encounters: Rethinking Access and Care in Digital Colonial Archives', *Archival Science*, vol. 19, 2019, pp. 141–165.
43. Yanni Alexander Loukissas, All Data Are Local: Thinking Critically in a Data-Driven Society, MIT Press, Cambridge, MA, 2019.
44. Myriah L. Cornwell and Lisa M. Campbell, 'Co-Producing Conservation and Knowledge: Citizen-Based Sea Turtle Monitoring in North Carolina, USA', *Social Studies of Science*, vol. 44, no. 1, 2012, p. 105.
45. Hauke Riesch and Clive Potter, 'Citizen Science as Seen by Scientists: Methodological, Epistemological and Ethical Dimensions', *Public Understanding of Science*, vol. 23, no. 1, 2014, pp. 107–120.
46. Finn Danielsen, Neil D. Burgess and Andrew Balmford, 'Monitoring Matters: Examining the Potential of Locally-Based Approaches', *Biodiversity and Conservation*, vol. 14, no. 11, 2005, pp. 2524–2542.
47. Ibid, p. 2527.
48. Compare with Susan Leigh Star, 'This Is Not a Boundary Object: Reflections on the Origin of a Concept", *Science, Technology, & Human Values*, vol. 35, no. 5, 2010, p. 607.
49. Jeffrey P. Cohn, 'Citizen Science: Can Volunteers do Real Research?', *BioScience*, vol. 58, no. 3, 2008, p. 194.
50. Compare with Kasperowski, Kullenberg and Rohden, 2020; Clotworthy 2019a; Clotworthy 2019b.
51. Compare with Minna Santaoja, 'Insect Affects: A Study on the Motivations of Amateur Entomologists and Implications for Citizen Science', *Science & Technology Studies*, vol. 35, no. 1, 2022, pp. 58–79.
52. Danielsen, Burgess and Balmford, 2005, p. 2524.
53. Compare with Pschetz and Bastian, 2018, p. 174.
54. Kimberly Christen and Jane Anderson, 'Toward Slow Archives', *Archival Science*, vol. 19, 2019, pp. 87–116.
55. Abeba Birhane et al., 'Power to the People? Opportunities and Challenges for Participatory AI', Paper presented at the Equity and Access in Algorithms, Mechanisms, and Optimization Conference, October 6–9, 2022, George Mason University, Arlington VA, USA

ARTICLE

The New Protectionism: Risk Aversion and Access to Indigenous Heritage Records

Nick Thieberger[1], Michael Aird[2], Clint Bracknell[3], Jason Gibson[4], Amanda Harris[5], Marcia Langton[6], Gaye Sculthorpe[7], and Jane Simpson[8]

[1]School of Languages and Linguistics, University of Melbourne; [2]Anthropology Museum, The University of Queensland, Brisbane; [3]Conservatorium of Music, UWA, Perth; [4]Alfred Deakin Institute, Deakin University, Burwood; [5]Sydney Conservatorium of Music, The University of Sydney; [6]Melbourne School of Population and Global Health, University of Melbourne; [7]Alfred Deakin Institute, Deakin University, Burwood; [8]ANU College of Arts and Social Sciences, Canberra

Abstract

This article discusses the problems encountered in accessing archival Indigenous language records, both by Indigenous people looking for information on their own languages and by non-Indigenous researchers supporting language work. It is motivated by Indigenous people not being able to access materials in archives, libraries, and museums that they need for heritage reasons, for personal reasons, or for revitalisation of language or cultural performance. For some of the authors, the experience of using Nyingarn, which aims to make manuscript language material available for re-use today, has been dispiriting, with what we term the 'new protectionism' preventing use of these materials.

Keywords: *Access blockage; ICIP; Australian Indigenous Languages*

[T]he task for linguists is to act as a channel to ensure that stolen knowledge and authority flow back to communities. (Lesley Woods)[1]

We write from several different positions and with a range of long-term experience as both Indigenous (Aird, Bracknell, Langton, Sculthorpe) and non-Indigenous (Thieberger, Gibson, Harris, Simpson) anthropologists, musicologists, and linguists.

To support Indigenous speakers and learners of Indigenous languages in the early 21st century a major contribution has to be access to all records of those languages. Many of these records have ended up, as accidents of history or by-products of colonial agendas, in widely dispersed holding institutions who now consider themselves the (de facto if not de jure) owners of that material. For holding institutions there is a delicate balance between their responsibilities in making collections accessible, and paying attention to the rights of Indigenous people whose information is represented in those collections. As Nicholls et al. point out, 'there is a move in

*Correspondence: Nick Thieberger, Email: thien@unimelb.edu.au

archival sciences to recognise the importance of engaging with Australian Indigenous communities in order to properly interpret and contextualise archival documents that include Indigenous language material'.[2] However, we observe that this move is not always facilitating access to these documents, and can, in fact, be doing the opposite, in what we call the new protectionism.

Many archival collections are held in institutions that are part of a colonial history, and that in the past have promoted free access to information, while prioritising the interests of copyright holders and depositors, as would be expected in state institutions. Such protection has been rightly criticised by Indigenous people who may, as a result, be denied access to materials made with their ancestors. As noticed by Anderson and Francis:

> Institutions that hold these collections and are now the copyright holders could behave differently, though: they could enact policy that relinquishes control, at least of the copyright, for the communities whose material it really is.[3]

The Aboriginal and Torres Strait Islander Library, Information and Resource Network (ATSILIRN) protocols of 1995 (updated 2012) set out principles for incorporating Indigenous perspectives under 12 major headings, and included the following (summarised for purposes of this article):

1.1 Recognise Aboriginal and Torres Strait Islanders as the traditional owners and custodians of Australia.

1.2 Ensure appropriate Aboriginal and Torres Strait Islander membership of governing and advisory bodies including boards, councils and committees.

12.1 Ensure sustainable choices of formats, descriptive methods and access and preservation strategies for Aboriginal and Torres Strait Islander peoples' knowledge, creativity and experience.

12.2 Pursue digitisation and digital access as a means of facilitating repatriation to Aboriginal and Torres Strait Islander communities, and preserving material for future generations.

12.4 Avoid providing access to items deemed secret, sacred or sensitive via their websites and online catalogues.

12.5 Ensure that material is digitised and stored electronically, in a manner consistent with and respectful to Aboriginal and Torres Strait Islander cultural protocols.

12.6 Work cooperatively with Aboriginal and Torres Strait Islander peoples to promote the creation, collection and management of digital materials.

12.7 Educate users of their collections about the potential benefits and risks of sharing digital content in an online environment.[4]

As can be seen, these protocols balance access (12.1, 12.2, 12.6) with restrictions based on sensitive materials (12.4, 12.5, 12.7). These protocols and others we will discuss here aimed to correct an earlier lack of consideration of Indigenous perspectives and rights in heritage materials held in archives and libraries.[5]

The following year, in May 1996, the Australian Society of Archivists (ASA) adopted a policy that noticed that archives may:

> contain information which is not known to Aboriginal people, which is regarded as secret/sacred by them, or which is presented in a manner which is offensive to them. Archives

and archivists need to be sensitive to these issues and to institute access policies which take account of the concerns and moral rights of Aboriginal people.⁶

Neither of these documents recommends restricting Indigenous peoples' access to archival collections, and each can be seen to be promoting general access that is based on an understanding of Indigenous content and any sensitivities known to be contained in the documents. They each present challenges to archives, calling on them to place Indigenous people at the centre of decisions made about their collections. Two of the ATSILIRN protocols (12.4 and 12.5) also prompt archives to handle sensitive and offensive content with extra care. In the ASA statement this need for caution is translated to a call for the implementation of suitable access policies. As we will show, the difficulties of implementing such policies in relation to collections that are incompletely or poorly described, and for which cultural owners may not have been identified, or for which there may be competing community interests, have led to policies that emphasise restriction at the expense of access.

The Tandanya Declaration of 2019 rightly situates archival collections as a problematic colonial legacy and sets out high-level principles for redressing the imbalance in control of material related to Indigenous peoples, including the 'need for affiliated Indigenous peoples to gain a degree of control over the access to information created by state-directed governance and cultural authorities'.⁷ It also notes 'that Indigenous social authority must participate as collaborators and co-authors in the description of records in the custody of public archival institutions whenever those records directly concern the identity of a particular Indigenous community'.⁸ We suggest that this collaboration can be enacted in digital collections with appropriate authentication systems. We outline some models of these below. We also notice that in large swathes of archival collections the identities of particular Indigenous communities can be unclear or misattributed, complicating the realisation of this principle.⁹

Moves to facilitate access to Indigenous items have been counterbalanced by new protection regimes in holding institutions that default to closing access in the absence of explicit permissions from Indigenous authorities. In the collective experience of the co-authors, this closing of access can occur even against the express wishes of the creator or copyright holder or of the Indigenous people they worked with who are recorded in the archived materials. This article calls for a renewed partnership between institutions, Indigenous language owners, researchers, and depositors, to overcome the problems caused by the new protectionism and aversion to risk.

Indigenous people have long been wanting access to material provided by their ancestors. As Henrietta Fourmile observed, 'Many people who have seen their family histories and photographs in Tindale's volumes have cried with joy, but there is also bitter resentment about the fact that we were never told about their existence'.[10]

Fourmile's heartfelt testimonial was written before the arrival of the internet. Today, much more language material is easily findable through the web, but much material still remains in archives, libraries, and museums without publicly accessible information about what language, people, place, and so on it includes. How can an Aboriginal person from Brewarrina, or Ramingining, or Kintore, find out what information about their families is held and in what institutions? And, even if they find out about it, travelling to a capital city or even to a regional centre like Alice Springs, is expensive. Barrowcliffe observes that 'Aboriginal and Torres Strait Islander peoples still struggle to access their records in large institutional archives' and that social media is filling a gap left by traditional institutions that are preventing access to heritage materials.[11] Often these social media postings include materials sourced from those institutions in the past but now shared freely and to the benefit of the very people who have the closest connection to those materials: family and members of the same cultural groups. Wilson and Barrowcliffe further note that the benefits of academic research have been 'hoarded' in a regime that protects the publisher but not the people represented in the work.[12]

In a detailed and moving description of her own efforts to access materials related to her immediate family, Brenda L Croft describes the 'bloody-minded 21st century rendition of paternalism and control'.[13] She also describes how a researcher, working through archival records, was able to locate a letter written by Croft's father, and to send her a copy of that letter. This was only possible because the letters were available for research, and copying was permitted, so that Croft could receive a copy. Increasingly, we are seeing this appropriate level of access being reduced. This is an example of a non-Aboriginal researcher finding and sharing information with Aboriginal community members, who otherwise would have never found this material. This highlights the problems each of the authors has experienced of some institutions greatly restricting access to non-Aboriginal researchers.

Another example of Indigenous people seeking information about their forebears is recounted by Smith et al. who observe that:

> The current situation undermines trust between Indigenous people and anthropologists. If the knowledge you impart to a researcher is likely to be kept from your descendants, why share it? The Berndt example demonstrates that intellectual property can be appropriated as soon as it is written down.[14]

Access to historic materials can support language revitalisation, cultural renewal, and relearning of ancestral practices. It can also be a source of pride in one's heritage. Once materials are accessible to communities, new metadata and transcriptions can be created that make the archival materials more useful, searchable, and able to be reproduced in pedagogical materials. We argue that it should be the role of holding institutions, and both Indigenous and non-Indigenous researchers to facilitate timely access for Indigenous people to existing sources that are records of a particular language or cultural practice.

Digitising materials and making catalogues accessible

Digitisation is a crucial step in accessibility, for example, as is recognised in the University of Sydney Library protocols:

> It is especially important that the Library encourages access to these materials by Aboriginal and Torres Strait Islander communities. Where possible, material will be digitised to facilitate access by those not based in Sydney. Digitisation work should emphasise material containing Aboriginal and Torres Strait Islander languages, songs, pictures of First Nations community members, and family histories......[15]

Digitised documents can be accessed remotely, removing the impediment of having to travel to a single location to view unique analog documents. But a digitised document is of little use if it is not clear who is being written about, what language groups they belong to, where the information was recorded, or what contextual information is needed to make sense of the material in the records. The University of Sydney Library protocols have this to say about making materials discoverable:

> To ensure First Nations perspectives are reflected in the cultural heritage collection, and to improve its accessibility and discoverability, the Library will continue to add descriptive metadata to items containing Aboriginal and Torres Strait Islander cultural materials. Descriptive metadata may include AIATSIS subject thesaurus headings, Austlang codes, cultural care notices and other contextual notes. The Library will add Austlang codes and

AIATSIS headings to new acquisitions, and where appropriate, and re-catalogue those items that have been recorded with unsuitable subject headings. The Library will seek to work with relevant communities to ensure that their knowledges are reflected in the classification and description of these materials. The Library will also promote appropriate classification and description in discussions with researchers, HDR students and potential authors who are working with First Nations communities and intending to deposit material into the collection.[16]

Making material accessible in this way is an enormous amount of work, and Gallery, Library, Archive, Museum (GLAM) institutions are rarely funded to carry it out. One or two Indigenous librarians are not enough to carry out the metadata management and updating, build connections with many Indigenous communities across Australia, discuss the contents of the material, and make their materials accessible to them. The lack of a pathway for making materials accessible and discoverable in a timely manner can, unfortunately, lead institutions to adopt policies that run counter to accessibility, resulting in the circular logic of material that is closed due to the lack of permissions, permissions which cannot be provided since the content of the documents is unknown, and content that can only be known if permission is given to view them.

Collecting institutions navigating the custodianship of cultural materials draw on 'a set of practices that recognize the entanglement of the two [Western and Indigenous knowledge] traditions as they move forward together in a somewhat problematic tension', which Nakata and Langton argue 'must be about developing trust and good working relations between Indigenous people and collecting institutions'.[17] Prior to the 1980s very few Indigenous researchers had ever accessed institutional collections. By the end of the 1980s this was starting to change, and this was also an era when photocopying technology became affordable and of a reasonable quality. These early photocopies obtained from libraries and museums soon became widely distributed within Aboriginal families and were quite often proudly displayed in photo albums and on the walls of homes. In recent decades, Aboriginal people have gained much expertise in researching institutional collections while also forming genuine relationships and sharing information with non-Aboriginal researchers. Technology has improved beyond photocopies; taking photos on phones and sharing digital files on the internet are now standard practice. Social media has emerged as an important way of distributing research outcomes within Aboriginal communities.[18]

There is a major problem when an Indigenous scholar wants to access archival materials related to their culture or language and finds an institution blocking that access. In the past, this was done because GLAM institutions and some of the researchers allied with them wanted to have privileged access themselves[19] for disciplinary or professional reasons[20] or because of concerns about exposure of sensitive cultural material or personal information.

Today access may be restricted because GLAM institutions don't have the in-house knowledge or the resources to consult the many different Indigenous groups across Australia whose materials are held in the institution. In many instances it may not be possible to find Indigenous people who are accepted by their communities as knowledgeable representatives for discussing the content of archival material, let alone what restrictions should be placed on it. Families may disagree about what material can be made public. Faced with the seeming impossibility of the task, and operating in a climate of concern about cultural safety and data sovereignty, in our experience, and that of colleagues we work with, GLAM institutions are clamping down on all access to material about Indigenous people unless their Indigenous staff members have cleared it for public access. Even when researchers have deposited material in public archives, community members many years later have often found it more time-effective to work with outsiders to track down the researcher and obtain copies from the researcher, rather than to wait for access through an institution.[21]

A relevant example is co-author Michael Aird's experience of identifying archival photographic images of Aboriginal people.[22] He notes that photographs held in the Pitt Rivers Museum (UK) of an Aboriginal man identified as coming from Western Australia are also held by the British Museum, the Macleay Museum and in a private collection. He was fortunate that all three institutions plus the private collector gave him access to their collections. This in turn enabled him to sort out that the photos were taken in Brisbane, not Western Australia.

While those institutions gave him access to their collections, other collecting institutions are moving towards preventing access to Aboriginal collections, unless written permission has been first obtained from Aboriginal communities. If Aird had been faced with this situation, he would have had to find a community in Western Australia to give permission to look at photos that were actually taken in Brisbane. This would have prevented him from ever figuring out where these photos were taken and passing that information on to Queensland Aboriginal people.

When he visits overseas museums or libraries, Aird tries to look at every Australian photo in their collection, in the hope of finding photos of Aboriginal people from south-east Queensland, his main research area. Within Australian institutional collections, looking at every Australian photo would be too large a job, so he would narrow that down to every photo from a particular region or every photo with Aboriginal content. In general, his research methods require that he look at as many photos as time permits. So policies that restrict the ability to look at photos based on an assumption that he can easily find Aboriginal community representatives to give permission greatly restricts his ability to carry out research and to supply the information to relevant communities.

Many materials are held in similar circumstances, with access denied even to Indigenous researchers related to the creators of the documents. Genevieve Campbell writes of her experience working with the Tiwi Strong Women's Group to get copies of recordings in the Australian Institute of Aboriginal and Torres Strait Islander Studies (AIATSIS):

> In April 2009 I was advised that the only way to have the material digitised and processed for release was to have Tiwi elders audition it to assess potential cultural restrictions. The material was not in line for digitisation because it had not had cultural restriction appraisal (which could only happen if the elders listened to it). This posed somewhat of a 'Catch 22' problem. The elders could not listen to it unless it was digitised and sent to the islands (in effect, released). With time stretching on, and potentially running out for older Tiwi people with direct interest in and knowledge of this material, it became imperative to the Tiwi elders that they take affirmative action.[23]

When the Tiwi elders travelled to Canberra to get access to copies of the recordings, they found almost all unavailable to them, as copyright holders could not be traced, and the institution pursued a lengthy process to deliver some of the files with institutional discretion eight months later.[24]

Moore et al. argue that:

> data are neglected things in research. Against commitments to care for research participants, the traces of research – interview transcripts, audio files, video, images, or material objects, and so on – which are also the traces of participants, appear as some of the 'neglected things' of research projects.[25]

When these data are cultural records there is an added imperative to care for them, and to ensure they can be made available to those involved in the research and their families.

Do it yourself archives

An emerging role for digital archiving has involved a new group of DIY[26] archivists recognising the value of records they and their colleagues produce, but, not seeing any institution capable of finding and receiving those records, they are making them available without a 'paternalistic research culture of risk avoidance'.[27] Given that the outcome of the compliance frameworks that government requires of most GLAM institutions can be restrictions on access to the very people these protectionist policies are intended to help, it is unsurprising that local and DIY solutions are sought. For example, there are local repositories of images, audio, and video managed using tools such as Ara Irititja,[28] Mukurtu,[29] Keeping Place,[30] and so on. Unfortunately, many of these are at risk of loss because there is no long-term repository supporting them.

The need for these DIY archives partly results from the absence of a means of accessing material in existing repositories, and partly in the definition of a 'suitable' repository. Universities often have 'repositories', but what is on offer is often data storage, not data curation. That is, files can be stored but are not provided with a public-facing catalogue or viewing system, and, consequently, have no licensing regime to make clear how the files can be used. The lack of a catalogue means they are not discoverable. 'Suitable' in the 21st century must include online access with licence conditions clearly set out, with a clear focus on providing access to Indigenous people rather than blocking access, or delaying access unreasonably.

A related problem is that some repositories (like AIATSIS) are not yet able to accept the rich digital assemblages created by people working on language or music documentation. These files require ways of viewing transcripts and media together, allowing searching through the text of the records. The model in some organisations is to split incoming material into audio, film, text and so on, based on an analog model in which these media needed distinct treatment. Limited cross-referencing (e.g. failure to link an audio file to a transcript of the file) makes material less accessible. Digital data allows re-integration of these datatypes, and also allows for much faster ingestion and delivery of files.

Examples of DIY archives working with Indigenous languages in Australia include the Living Archive of Aboriginal Languages (LAAL),[31] the Pacific and Regional Archive for Digital Sources in Endangered Cultures (PARADISEC),[32] and the recently developed Nyingarn[33] (each discussed further below).[34]

The LAAL is a digital archive of endangered literature in Australian Indigenous languages of the Northern Territory. It contains nearly 4,000 books in 50 languages from 40 communities available to read online or download freely.[35] Cathy Bow wrote candidly about the conundrums faced by the LAAL where it was not always possible to determine from whom permissions should be sought. This had the result that:

> The public website includes only records and documents with appropriate permissions, whereas the metadata of records which have been scanned but are not publicly available is hidden within the system, only visible to members of the project team and technical support staff ... This results in the paradox that the more unidentified materials are made available online, the easier it is to identify them and get permission; but the materials cannot be put online without appropriate permission. Returning to first principles of communication, consultation, and consent, it is difficult to share information about works that can't yet be made public without making them public.[36]

PARADISEC was established in 2003 to make records of Pacific materials that were held by researchers in Australia available to the people recorded.[37] It has always been a standards-compliant digital collection and focuses on finding and exposing records with whatever licences are required by the depositors. Access can be provided instantly to authorised users, and private items can be shared with a nominated set of users even if items are not otherwise publicly available. A takedown principle is available to users, but has never been requested in the 20 years of PARADISEC's operation. PARADISEC's digital platform can operate with minimal staffing, and material deposited one day can be available for access the next day.

Another example is Nyingarn, which is a platform that provides a secure online environment in which Indigenous language manuscripts can be read as text and searched. A reason for building Nyingarn is that manuscripts are often held in GLAM institutions, far from home communities, usually with a high literacy bar to using a catalogue, and requiring attendance at the institution to look at the papers. For example, in a precursor to Nyingarn and in a collaboration with the National Library of Australia (NLA), the 24,000 pages of Daisy Bates' questionnaire of vocabularies from 1904,[38] mainly from Western Australia, is now online, searchable and available for all kinds of new uses.[39] This work contains information from many Aboriginal people, in a number of different Indigenous languages, and has been overwhelmingly well received by Aboriginal people who find ancestral information in it. However, this project would simply be impossible to carry out under the current protectionist policy of most holding institutions.

Nyingarn provides a workspace in which manuscripts can be transcribed, keeping the original page image together with the transcript to allow correction and verification of the transcript. While in the workspace, the manuscript is available only to the user and their nominated collaborators. The Nyingarn workspace lists users who are permitted to see each item, as determined by the depositor of the item. They can then work to transcribe and then download the text of the document and to enrich the metadata description of it. This enriched version can be given back to the institution that holds the original manuscript, adding to their catalogue and making the document easier to find for others. Nyingarn also provides a repository in which finished documents can be released, subject to permissions provided by the relevant language authority.[40] Creating textual versions of manuscripts can then assist in determining access, for example, when some parts of a manuscript may require restricted access, but most of the manuscript can be available more generally. In this way, access for language programmes can be provided while avoiding any material that needs to be treated with more care. AIATSIS is a partner in the Nyingarn project and will maintain the platform to provide access to manuscripts in Australian Indigenous languages.

Nyingarn is now an extensible platform in which new manuscripts can be added, transcribed, and re-used in current cultural programmes. It has proven its value by having had some 900 manuscripts uploaded and having champions among those who have been able, for the first time, to organise and access manuscripts in their languages.

Despite having a number of State libraries, AIATSIS, and the NLA as partners in the Nyingarn funding application, each of these agencies has been unable to provide manuscripts for use in Nyingarn or has only been able to do so after a lengthy series of meetings. The time to prepare and access a document at one of these institutions can be 6 months from the moment of application. While understaffing and archaic processes account for some of this delay, there is also a layer of risk aversion that prevents access. In working with speakers to attempt to obtain manuscripts and having a number of letters from relevant language authorities approving their access furnished to the holding institution, we have been told by those institutions that they are not signed by the correct authorities.

In other cases, institutions have declined making manuscripts available for digitisation by the Nyingarn Project because the archive is planning a process of community consultation. However, in cases of large collections such as those of A. P. Elkin and R. H. Mathews who worked across many language groups, it is not always clear which languages are represented in the collection. Sometimes when languages are identified in the original source, they have been coded by the archive using inconsistent language names.

An example is an item in the University of Sydney Archives titled 'Various Notes and Vocabularies'[41] in the collection of A. P. Elkin. The descriptive note for this item mentions the following languages: Dharawal, Dharug, Eora, Dunghutti, Gandangara, Kamilaroi, Kattang, and Awabakal. But a search using the Archives' search tool for the Elkin collection, which provides the option to search either by place or by Austlang language code, returns this item only for the first five languages named, and not the last three (and only if the user selects 'Dharug language', for example, from the dropdown list and not 'Dharug people'). The Archives' collection is only discoverable via their search tool, and the item does not turn up in a search of Trove records on Elkin, meaning potential users have to already know about the collection and its location. This not only makes it challenging for a community user to discover that records in their language are held in the archive, but obtaining community permission for making these records accessible presents a potentially insurmountable challenge (due to both the large number of languages documented in this single archival item, and contemporary community politics of language ownership). By not digitising and making the notes and vocabularies available, archives can put themselves in the position of arbiter of intra-community disputes, in which they have no authority to arbitrate. We suggest that the language data should be made findable and accessible as a priority, and that a paternalistic approach to guarding the data can exacerbate, not defuse these kinds of disagreements and disputes.

The Howitt and Fison project[42] (2017–2020) contains transcriptions of original notes and papers of Gippsland magistrate Alfred W. Howitt and Methodist missionary Lorimer Fison. In this project, the material that was sourced from multiple collections (the State Library of Victoria, Museums Victoria, and St. Marks Theological College) went through an extensive community consultation process that resulted in the records being made available online, via a site hosted by Museums Victoria. The project was partly inspired by the *Spencer and Gillen* website, which featured page-aligned transcriptions of the fieldnotes and collections made by the anthropologists Walter Baldwin Spencer and Frank Gillen.[43] For the Howitt and Fison project, transcriptions of these articles were made by the project team, Indigenous community members and non-Indigenous volunteers.[44] These transcriptions transformed previously inaccessible and hard to read manuscripts into rich and usable cultural heritage and language resources. Any material identified by communities as being culturally restricted or sensitive, such as Howitt's notes on Yuin male initiations, were not included online. This site would be a prized example within any collecting institution that valued making material accessible for Indigenous people. It is, however, at risk of being lost due to the incoming policy of risk aversion that demands that community permissions must be evidenced for the entire collection, which in this case pertains to over 100 different language and cultural groups across southeastern and inland Australia.

DIY archives are often driven by an awareness of the imperative to balance risk with the importance of caring for and making cultural heritage materials available. The three collections discussed above (LAAL, PARADISEC, Nyingarn) use a takedown principle that invites feedback on material that may need to be restricted, which allows more material to be openly available than is the case in other collections. The library sector has had 'takedown' policies in place for a long time now[45] and this approach appears to have balanced the imperative of access with community concerns and interests. In the same vein, Moore et al. characterise their decision to keep rather than to hide data as:

> a feminist ethic of care. Against a culture of risk avoidance, we argue that research, and care, always involve risk. We suggest that an inventive feminist ethic of care-full risk, understood as responsible action [..], allows us to take seriously matters of accountability.[46]

Making material accessible

Established GLAM institutions are struggling with determining how to assign access rights in Indigenous materials. They are often uncertain about what Indigenous materials their collections contain and they are concerned to provide a kind of ownership of some rights in those materials to appropriate parties. If that sounds a little vague, it is because an issue for these institutions is how to determine which Indigenous communities have interests in materials they hold, who within those communities can decide on those rights, and how to adjudicate differences within groups who may have an interest, or between a range of groups who may all have an interest in materials whose subjects cover a number of different locations or cultural groups.

The travelling corroboree known variously as '*wanji wanji*' and '*laka*' offers a compelling example of how material in archives can intersect with many diverse Indigenous cultural and linguistic groups. The podcast series 'Song With No Boss' features interviews with Aboriginal people across Western Australia, the Northern Territory and South Australia discussing how essentially the same song, *wanji wanji*, came to be freely performed by men and women across more than half of the continent.[47] While interviewees describe the song as being well-known and shared across regions, most are amazed and overjoyed as they listen to recordings of performances from many thousands of kilometres away. Indigenous and non-Indigenous researchers were only able to identify just how incredibly far this 'entertainment' song had spread by comparing archival material and contemporary recordings of performances from different areas across Australia.[48] Moves to further restrict access to archival material under false assumptions that everything in collections should be cordoned off and 'owned' by nebulous regional Indigenous corporations underestimate the dynamic and sophisticated ways Indigenous peoples have long shared language and performance repertoires across vast distances.

When it is unclear which Indigenous people were involved in providing information, for example in a vocabulary collected in the 1800s, the default position in some institutions is to close access until the right people can be found. If that manuscript has not been transcribed it is difficult to work with, and it may need the expertise of someone who knows about Australian languages and can identify where it is likely to be from in the first place before current speakers of the language can be identified. However, GLAM institutions often do not know how to find such experts. If relevant researchers (Indigenous or non-Indigenous) are not given access, then it is likely that the materials will remain inaccessible because the GLAM institution will not be able to catalogue the material so that it becomes discoverable.[49] An alternative is to decide that it is to the benefit of the very people in whose best interests the institution claims to be acting to make the material available, with suitable notices and policies in place to take it down should it be problematic (cf. what Moore et al. call 'care-full risk').[50] This approach enables communities of interest to interact with collections and inform decisions rather than leaving these judgements to an institution.

Timely access to materials capitalises on a moment where the information may be important for a current project, with a particular set of people involved, both of which may dissipate over time. If it will take 6 months to get access, the reason for wanting access may have passed, or, more seriously, older people who can comment on early sources may no longer be alive. The importance of many early manuscripts to descendants of the people originally providing information is that the documents can jog memories, or provide new information for use in language or cultural revitalisation programmes. As Nicholls et al. observe, in their consultations about access to collections, 'many community members discussed the value of material and its ability to join the past to the future'.[51] This is especially the case in places where Indigenous languages have not been spoken for some time, and the records – when properly deciphered – can provide invaluable information for current language work.

The new protectionism

There is a very great risk that the new protectionism will inhibit the deposit of valuable materials into an archive, so that, paradoxically, the very records made now and in the past generation, that should be most amenable to digital transfer and curation, are at risk of loss. This is exacerbated if the same protectionist policies are now requiring permissions from someone other than the creator of the records for deposit. It is unlikely that the desired outcome is the loss of the records, but it is the likely outcome.

By taking a protectionist approach to their collections in an effort to redress their role in supporting colonialism, GLAM institutions risk taking backward steps and preventing their collections from being available for decolonial revitalisation work today. The availability of collections for community access and potential revitalisation work can be imperilled by policies that aim to guard against misuse. Increased protectionism is often a response to calls to recognise Indigenous Cultural and Intellectual Property (ICIP).[52] But if not held in balance with making collections discoverable and accessible to those with rights to them, the risk-averse approach to ICIP only perpetuates colonial and paternalistic approaches by positioning the institution as arbiter of access, rather than the community and cultural custodians. As a result, institutions responding to calls for greater attention to the needs of Indigenous communities may block access to those who should have it. The Indigenous Archives Collective articulated six principles on the Right of Reply to Indigenous Knowledges and Information held in Archives:

1. The Right to Know
2. Participation
3. Cultural Safety
4. Consent
5. Institutions as Facilitators not Owners
6. Advocacy.[53]

An emphasis only on the Collective's principles 3 and 4, may result in risk-averse policies that imperil goals 1, 2, and 5. In particular, policies such as that of the NLA[54] to implement new ICIP protocols by limiting access to viewing at the library only,[55] and not through open access online tools such as the Howitt and Fison project and Nyingarn, are hard to reconcile with the Collective's Principle 5:

> Paradigms of institutional 'ownership' of materials should shift to responsibilities associated with custodianship and facilitation of access, interpretations and mediated use of these collections led by and in collaboration with Indigenous peoples.[56]

We have responded to relevant NLA ICIP guiding principles[57] in Table 1.

Table 1 Response to NLA ICIP protocols

NLA ICIP protocol	Author response
4. Free, Prior, Informed Consent: The Library is committed to ensuring that the free, prior informed consent of First Nations peoples is obtained before using or authorising use of ICIP where possible to do so	As outlined elsewhere in this article, it can be impossible to get consent for material with unknown content. An institution like the NLA should be in a position to provide access in a secure environment so that experts (e.g., speakers of the languages or researchers familiar with these people and their languages) can determine what language is likely to be represented and whether there is any material that should be restricted. The default should always be to make material available to speakers rather than restricting access
5. Interpretation and Cultural Integrity: The Library supports the right of First Nations peoples to be the primary guardians and interpreters of their ICIP. The Library seeks to ensure that its interpretations of ICIP are respectful of the cultural integrity of that material	Again, the issue here is who is to determine who are the guardians of the material if the contents of the material are not accessible and understandable and if different groups have interests in the same material. ICIP is a collective property and we are concerned that in principle permission would be required not only from the individual Indigenous creator but also from some un-defined 'community'.
7. Attribution: First Nations peoples are custodians of their ICIP and have the right to be attributed in relation to their ICIP. The Library commits to acknowledging First Nations peoples in relation to their ICIP and any use of their ICIP	This is appropriate, but raises the same issue, that is, who is to be attributed if materials are not transcribed and their content is not understood
8. Benefit Sharing: The Library acknowledges the right of First Nations peoples to benefit from the sharing of their ICIP and culture	This is appropriate, but the problem is that the NLA wants to determine who can share and access material so that it is the arbiter, and blocker, rather than the provider of the benefit to Indigenous people that this protocol advocates

NLA, National Library of Australia; ICIP, Indigenous Cultural and Intellectual Property.

Thorpe and Booker point out that '[w]hile some institutions recognise the importance of their collections for language and cultural revitalisation there is still limited research and dialogue relating to truth-telling and the need for libraries to recognise their roles in supporting colonialism'.[58] At the moment in history when these institutions could be supporting cultural reaffirmation by offering their holdings to Indigenous people, with digitisation allowing increased access, they are caught in a protectionist paradigm that prevents access (supporting colonialism in Thorpe and Booker's terms). In part this is also due to inefficient internal processes that do not allow quick and easy access to holdings, requiring manual handling and delays. The layers of permissions required make it hard to distinguish concerns over ICIP from institutional inertia, and, further, using ICIP as the excuse for not giving materials to people whose ICIP is represented in the materials just compounds the problem.

The current situation is idiosyncratic and inconsistent in application. It is often the case that archival material from one collector is held in different institutions due to the changing organisational affiliation of a researcher over the course of their career. It is not uncommon for different protocols to apply in each or depending on the staff member on the day. We have experienced cases of not being allowed access to a book in one archive but given access to it in another (in the same city). Similarly, cultural materials or objects may be held in one institution and associated documentation of those materials is held in another.[59] In a recent instance, one institution was unable to give another government institution corrected archival documentation about objects held in the other, as the policies of the new protectionism insist that the archival information can only be given to an Indigenous person. This means that the material in the first institution continues to be curated, researched, and accessed by Indigenous communities with incorrect and incomplete documentation, severely disadvantaging Indigenous knowledge discovery.

A welcome development is the growing numbers of Indigenous staff in archives and collecting institutions. However, risk-averse policies also place an unreasonable burden on those individuals, who may be able to provide specialist advice and have access to wide networks of other Indigenous people, but who are not able to speak for Aboriginal and Torres Strait Islander communities across the country.

There is plentiful evidence that careful research in collections can result in new information with important cultural and social impacts. The work done on the Howitt and Fison project, for example, led to the discovery of placenames for the Melbourne area that have now been taken up by the Wurundjeri Woi-wurrung Aboriginal Corporation and others to celebrate Indigenous history and identity in the city.[60] This research was based on a long process of transcribing Howitt's difficult handwriting to find small details of invaluable information interspersed within notes relating to numerous Indigenous cultural groups from across Australia. Similarly, the rediscovery of a ceremonial ground[61] in Victoria was the result of collaborative work on these papers by a non-Indigenous anthropologist and Gunaikurnai descendants of the people who worked with Howitt in the 1880s.[62] These discoveries, which have had significant benefit to Indigenous communities, were only possible because the project enabled exploratory research across collections that were pertinent to many different Australian Indigenous groups. Howitt's papers often include references to multiple groups and languages in one document. Seeking approval from all of the relevant groups for a single item is impractical.

A subsidiary reason for access to historic materials is to test and potentially correct misinformation in the public domain. An example from David Nash (pc) involves chasing up the etymology of the topographic term *cowal* borrowed into English, which can be found in the standard current Wiradjuri dictionary:

gawal 'a valley, a plate'[63]

This is helpfully sourced to (G) i.e. Günther – where on page 85 is the entry

Gawal—a plat, a valley[64]

This calls for checking against the several Günther manuscripts archived in various places.[65] Figure 1 & 2 from Günther's 1837–40 'Lecture' show that the printer read script F as P, with corroboration from other instances of script F and P: So the gloss should be 'flat' not 'plat' or 'plate'.

Figure 1. Günther 1840 MS, page 278: "Gawal, Flat, valley."[66]

(Related is the entry 'Gnrra- a plate, a dish' with the printer's error of n for u, readily corrected since in the alphabetical list it occurs between Guron and Gurrabang).[67]

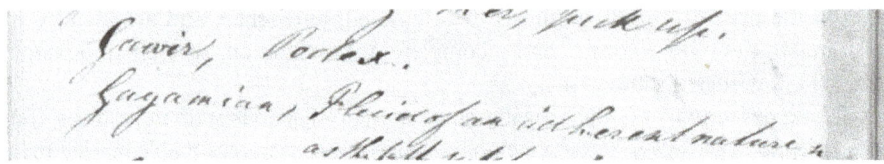

Figure 2. Günther 1840 MS page 278: "Gawir, Podex." illustrating P, and "Gayamian, Fluid of an adherent nature" illustrating F.

At the time the Günther manuscripts weren't online; these extracts were found on microfilm at AIATSIS, a collection which is now less accessible after all microforms were moved to an AIATSIS storage facility in Mitchell where researchers aren't allowed. Bookings to view and access material in the AIATSIS Collection must be made two weeks in advance.[68]

Resourcing Indigenous access to records

Inadequate funding, staffing, appropriate knowledge management, and technology in the GLAM sector institutions often limit the access of Indigenous people seeking records about their family histories, historical events, language resources, and cultural materials. Without the capacity to effectively provide adequate access to and online information about these collections, the result is misrepresentation and underrepresentation of Indigenous voices, and collections that are not discoverable or accessible to communities of origin. By committing resources, institutions can ensure culturally sensitive access and curation, engage in meaningful community consultation, and foster cross-cultural understanding and appreciation. Meaningful community consultation is lacking and has become a major issue for Indigenous people searching for records pertaining to their languages and family lines and also for Indigenous researchers.

At the *Implementing Indigenous Data Licensing and Access: Empowering Communities and Upholding Cultural Rights* roundtable event in Brisbane on the 5th and 6th July 2023 which several of this article's authors attended, Indigenous researchers, librarians and curators described their encounters with the new protectionism: non Indigenous curators tell them to 'get a letter from your community', or 'get a letter from your elder'. In at least one case, the researcher asking was the relevant 'elder' but the institutional gate-keeper refused to accept this. Curators may have no knowledge of the 'community' they might be referring to in any instance, nor the nature of these 'communities', disrupted by history as they are, with some historical residents and large diasporas from the apical ancestors who lived elsewhere. Moreover, 'elders' are often young, reflecting the mortality rates in Indigenous communities. The 'communities' and 'elders' that these curators refer to are figments of their imagination. It has become urgent that the access processes and protocols are revised by expert Indigenous researchers, curators, and librarians to ensure that the GLAM sector staff are not denying access as a result of their own ignorance or – as is more likely the case – their fears of dealing in more complex ways with representatives of families, clans, communities or social groups who desire access to records for a range of legitimate reasons. The representatives who approach the institutions are, more often than not, the highly educated, literate members of their families, and the kind of verification that institutions demand does not reflect the exigencies of families, family lines, and other social groupings whose members desire and need access to the records to support their quest for rights, such as native title rights, family reunification, historical representation and reclamation of their language heritage.

Many of the records discussed in this article are held in libraries, museums, and archives, sometimes with catalogue entries that identify which language is included, but more often with little or no information about the Indigenous language included in the record. There are several aspects that need to be addressed to enable Indigenous people to locate these records. First, the catalogue or finding aid has to be online, ideally also available via the NLA's Trove, to maximise findability. Second, the catalogue has to identify what languages or cultural group identifiers are in the manuscript and to use a standard descriptor, like the Austlang codes[69] managed by the AIATSIS (to avoid the problem of multiple spellings of language names). Third, the text of the manuscript should be searchable, to allow speakers to locate people, places, or terms that will be of use in their language programs. If these conditions can be met it will allow the communities that Woods refers to (above) to find and determine what should happen with historical manuscripts in their languages.

We suggest that GLAM institutions should:

- Err on the side of making material available to Indigenous people
- Digitise records for access
- Build platforms for presentation of digital records
- Provide an efficient and accessible takedown mechanism
- Invest in providing online accurate descriptions of the language content of material
- Have clear access conditions attached to items, based on informed consideration of their content (predicated on the earlier steps)
- Provide timely access to material
- Make it easy for legacy[70] material to be deposited in archives

Conclusions

We observe that records of Indigenous knowledge are becoming increasingly difficult for Indigenous people and other researchers to access due to a new protectionism in holding institutions that is often well-intentioned, but that results in a lack of access to valuable primary records. We suggest that the role of such publicly funded institutions must be to facilitate timely access to historical records, especially for the people most closely associated with the content of these records.

We have emphasised issues with accessing language data held in cultural institutions; however, many of the same issues also apply to accessing cultural objects in collections and the associated documentation held in museum archives. The lack of online databases makes finding ancestral belongings extremely difficult for community members for the same reasons outlined above for language materials. Few cultural institutions appear to be implementing the recommendations made in Terri Janke's roadmap for the Australian Museums and Galleries Association (AMAGA), which include providing online inventories of items in collections, for example:

> Organisations must address inventory and access to collections by Indigenous people. Where the works are unprovenanced, and details unknown, research and identification work should take place in a coordinated approach following cultural protocols. This should be explored using a variety of methods, especially digital technology.[71]

We have offered several examples of collections of heritage cultural material that have been made available for digitisation, rendering as text (via OCR or transcription) and provided by a secure online system to authorised users in order to identify contents and then to make informed decisions about access to that material. This should reduce the workload on institutions wanting to make this material available. We recognise that there is a great deal of this material and it needs to be accessed and enriched in a timely manner by those most intimately involved with it, the people recorded and their descendants.

Disclosure statement

Bracknell, Simpson, and Thieberger are Chief Investigators in the Nyingarn project. Harris, Simpson, and Thieberger are Chief Investigators in PARADISEC. Gibson is a Chief Investigator in the Howitt and Fison project. Langton is a Chief Investigator on a grant from the Australian Research Data Commons for the improving Indigenous Research Capability project and a grant from the National Indigenous Affairs Agency for the Community Data Projects. Thieberger and Harris are Chief Investigators in the Language Data Commons of Australia.

Acknowledgements

The authors would like to thank Linda Barwick, Sophie Lewincamp, Amanda Lourie, Stephen Morey, David Nash, Joanna Sassoon, and referees for information that has improved this article.

Funding for work referred to in this article came from:

ARC Linkage Infrastructure, Equipment and Facilities (LIEF), 'Modularised cultural heritage archives future-proofing PARADISEC', (LE220100010); ARDC HASS Research Data Commons and Indigenous Research Capability Program, 'Developing the Linguistics Data Commons of Australia', 2022–24; Nyingarn: a platform for primary sources in Australian Indigenous languages (ARC LIEF grant no. LE210100013).

We declare that we have no conflicts of interest.

Notes

1. Lesley Woods, Something's Gotta Change. Redefining Collaborative Linguistic Research, ANU Press, Canberra, 2023. https://doi.org/10.22459/SGC.2022
2. Sophie Nicholls, Lauren Booker, Kirsten Thorpe, Melissa Jackson, Clement Girault, Ronald Briggs, and Caroline Jones, 'From Principle to Practice: Community Consultation Regarding Access to Indigenous Language Material in Archival Records at the State Library of New South Wales', Archives and Manuscripts, vol. 44, no. 3, 2016, pp. 110–23. https://doi.org/10.1080/01576895.2016.1239116.
3. Jane Anderson and James E. Francis, 'Decolonial Futures of Sharing: "Protecting Our Voice," Intellectual Property, and Penobscot Nation Language Materials', in Adrianna Link, Abigail Shelton, and Patrick Spero (eds.), Indigenous Languages and the Promise of Archives, University of Nebraska Press, Lincoln, NE, 2021, pp. 31–62. https://doi.org/10.2307/j.ctv1k03s31.8.
4. https://atsilirn.aiatsis.gov.au/protocols.php.
5. In 1989 the World Archaeological Inter-Congress adopted an accord which recognised that 'the concerns of various ethnic groups, as well as those of science are legitimate and to be respected' (https://worldarch.org/code-of-ethics/). This was the Vermillion Accord on Human Remains, which led to the United States Government introducing the Native American Graves Protection and Repatriation Act in 1990 (https://www.nps.gov/subjects/nagpra/index.htm). This legislation has had a major influence on collecting institutions and how they respectfully work with Indigenous communities. See Cressida Fforde, Jane Hubert, and Paul Turnbull, The Dead and Their Possessions: Repatriation in Principle, Policy, and Practice, Routledge, London, 2002.
6. https://www.archivists.org.au/documents/item/32.
7. International Council on Archives Expert Matters Indigenous Group, Tandanya – Adelaide Declaration, 2019, available at https://www.naa.gov.au/sites/default/files/2020-06/Tandanya-Adelaide-Declaration.pdf, 4(a).
8. Ibid, 3(b).
9. For a nuanced discussion of the balance between Indigenous rights and issues of institutional access see Linda Barwick, Jennifer Green, Petronella Vaarzon-Morel, and Katya Zissermann, 'Conundrums and Consequences: Doing Archival Returns in Australia', in Linda Barwick, Jennifer Green, and Petronella Vaarzon-Morel (eds.), Archival Returns: Central Australia and Beyond, LD&C Special Publication 18, University of Hawai'i Press & Sydney University Press, Honolulu, HI & Sydney, pp. 1–27, available at http://hdl.handle.net/10125/24875/.

10. Henrietta Fourmile, 'Who Owns the Past? Aborigines as Captives of the Archives', Aboriginal History, vol. 13, 1989, pp. 1–8. http://doi.org/10.22459/AH.13.2011p.3.
11. Rose Barrowcliffe, 'The Future of Australian Indigenous Records and Archives is Social', in Bronwyn Carlson, Madi Day, Sandy O'Sullivan, and Tristan Kennedy (eds.), The Routledge Handbook of Australian Indigenous Peoples and Futures, Routledge, London, 2023, pp. 367–77.
12. Leann Wilson (Bidjara) and Rose Barrowcliffe (Butchulla), 'Green Ribbon and Blue Ribbon Stories: Applying a Bidjara Way of Knowing to Understanding Records', Archives and Manuscripts, vol. 50, no. 2, 2022, p. 44. https://doi.org/10.37683/asa.v50.10921.
13. Brenda L. Croft, Sandy Toussaint, Felicity Meakins, and Patrick McConvell, 'For the Children …': Aboriginal Australia, Cultural Access, and Archival Obligation', in Linda Barwick, Jennifer Green, and Petronella Vaarzon-Morel (eds.), Archival Returns: Central Australia and Beyond, LD&C Special Publication 18, University of Hawai'i Press and Sydney University Press, Honolulu, HI and Sydney, 2019, p. 187.
14. Claire Smith, Gary Jackson, Geoffrey Gray, and Vincent Copley, 'Who Owns a Family's Story? Why It's Time to Lift the Berndt Field Notes Embargo', The Conversation, September 2018, available at https://theconversation.com/friday-essay-who-owns-a-familys-story-why-its-time-to-lift-the-berndt-field-notes-embargo-94652.
15. University of Sydney Library and Nathan Sentence, Aboriginal and Torres Strait Islander Cultural Protocols, University of Sydney, Sydney, 2021, §3.4. https://doi.org/10.25910/hrdq-9n85.
16. Ibid §3.8.
17. Martin Nakata and Marcia Langton, 'Introduction', in Martin Nakata and Marcia Langton (eds.), Australian Indigenous Knowledge and Libraries, UTS Press, Sydney, 2006, pp. 3–6.
18. Michael Aird, 'From Illustration to Evidence: The Evidential Value of Photographs in Native Title', Presentation at the Australian Society of Archivists Conference, 2021; see also Barrowcliffe, 'The Future of Australian Indigenous Records'. See footnote 11.
19. Michael F. Brown, Who Owns Native Culture? Harvard University Press, Santa Fe, NM, 2009; Linda Tuhiwai Smith, Decolonizing Methodologies: Research and Indigenous Peoples, Zed Books, London, 2013; Jason Gibson, Ceremony Men: Making Ethnography and the Return of the Strehlow Collection, State University of New York Press, Albany, NY, 2020.
20. Mike Jones, Artefacts, Archives, and Documentation in the Relational Museum, Routledge, Abingdon, 2021.
21. Jan Turner, 'Dr Cool and His Leading Lady: The Legacy of the Goulds' Work at Patjarr', Journal of the Anthropological Society of South Australia, vol. 45, 2021, p. 58, available at https://anthropologicalsoci-etysa.com/s/JASSA-45-Turner-e-copy.pdf.
22. Aird, 'From Illustration to Evidence'. See footnote 18.
23. Genevieve Campbell, 'Song as Artefact: The Reclaiming of Song Recordings: Empowering Indigenous Stakeholders—And the Recordings Themselves', in Amanda Harris (ed.), Circulating Cultures: Exchanges of Australian Indigenous Music, Dance and Media, ANU Press, Canberra, 2014, p. 105.
24. Ibid., p. 108.
25. Niamh Moore, Nikki Dunne, Martina Karels, and Mary Hanlon, 'Towards an Inventive Ethics of Carefull Risk: Unsettling Research through DIY Academic Archiving', Australian Feminist Studies, vol. 36, no. 108, p. 184. https://doi.org/10.1080/08164649.2021.2018991.
26. DIY = Do it yourself.
27. Moore et al., 'Towards and Inventive Ethics', p. 183.
28. https://irititja.com.
29. https://mukurtu.org.
30. https://thekeepingplace.com.
31. Catherine Bow, Michael Christie, and Brian Devlin, 'Developing a Living Archive of Aboriginal Languages', Language Documentation & Conservation, vol. 8, no. 345, 2014, p. 360, available at http://hdl.handle.net/10125/24612.
32. https://paradisec.org.au.
33. Nyingarn (https://nyingarn.net) is a platform for converting images of manuscripts to text, focussed on manuscripts of Australian Indigenous languages. It is an Australian Research Council funded project (2022–2024) in which a number of libraries and AIATSIS are partners. It will be housed at AIATSIS from mid-2024.
34. It must be emphasised that a DIY archive in this sense is still an archive: it conforms to relevant standards and makes provision for the longevity of the objects it creates. These are NOT simply websites and we are

very concerned to make the point that a website on its own is not an archive, as discussed in Thieberger's blog from 2017, https://www.paradisec.org.au/blog/2017/11/a-website-is-not-an-archive/.
35. The description is taken from the LAAL website: https://livingarchive.cdu.edu.au.
36. Catherine Bow and Patricia Hepworth, 'Observing and Respecting Diverse Knowledge Traditions in a Digital Archive of Indigenous Language Materials', Journal of Copyright in Education and Librarianship, vol. 3, no. 1, 2019, pp. 17, 20. https://doi.org/10.17161/jcel.v3i1.7485
37. Nick Thieberger, 'Technology in Support of Languages of the Pacific: Neo-Colonial or Post-Colonial?' Asian-European Music Research Journal, vol. 5, no. 3, 2020, pp. 17–24. https://doi.org/10.30819/aemr.5-3.
38. https://bates.org.au.
39. Nick Thieberger, 'Daisy Bates in the Digital World', in Peter K. Austin, Harold Koch, and Jane Simpson (eds.), Language, Land and Song: Studies in Honour of Luise Hercus, EL Publishing, London, 2016, pp. 102–114. http://www.elpublishing.org/docs/6/01/LLS-Chapter-08-Thieberger.pdf
40. The language authority is taken to be the person doing the most work on their language. If differing opinions are expressed by such potential authorities we will negotiate and take down the items if necessary.
41. https://uniarchivesonline.sydney.edu.au/#/records/item/72019?src=map.
42. https://howittandfison.org.
43. Philip Batty and Jason Gibson, 'Reconstructing the Spencer and Gillen Collection Online: Museums, Indigenous Perspectives and the Production of Cultural Knowledge in the Digital Age', in Holger Meyer, Christoph Schmitt, Alf-Christian Shering, and Stephanie Janssen (eds.), Corpora Ethnographica Online Strategien der Digitalisierung kultureller Archive und ihrer Präsentation im Internet, Waxman, Munster, 2014, pp. 29–48.
44. Rachel Hendery and Jason Gibson, 'Crowdsourcing Downunder', KULA: Knowledge Creation, Dissemination, and Preservation Studies, vol. 3, no. 1, 2019, pp. 1–12. https://doi.org/10.5334/kula.52. See footnote 11.
45. Martin Nakata, Gabrielle Gardiner, Jason Gibson, Jill McKeough, Alex Byrne, and Vicky Nakata, 'Indigenous Digital Collections: An Early Look at the Organisation and Culture Interface', Australian Academic and Research Libraries, vol. 39, no. 4, 2008, pp. 223–36.
46. Moore et al., 'Towards an Inventive Ethics', p. 181.
47. Daniel Browning, Myfany Turpin, and Clint Bracknell, 'Song with No Boss', ABC Radio National Five-Part Podcast Series, 2022. https://www.abc.net.au/listen/programs/awaye/song-with-no-boss-episode one/101612960.
48. Myfany Turpin, Brenda Croft, Clint Bracknell, and Felicity Meakins, 'Aboriginal Australia's Smash Hit that Went Viral', The Conversation, 20 March 2019, available at https://theconversation.com/aboriginal-australias-smash-hit-that-went-viral-112615.
49. Each of the authors has experienced this situation but we cannot go into details out of respect for the institutions involved.
50. Moore et al., 'Towards an Inventive Ethics'.
51. Nicholls et al., 'From Principle to Practice', p. 115.
52. https://www.terrijanke.com.au/post/Indigenous-data-sovereignty-the-legal-and-cultural-considerations.
53. Indigenous Archives Collective, 'The Indigenous Archives Collective Position Statement on the Right of Reply to Indigenous Knowledges and Information Held in Archives', Archives and Manuscripts, vol. 49, no. 3, 2021, pp. 247–8. https://indigenousarchives.net/indigenous-archives-collective-position-statement-on-the-right-of-reply-to-indigenous-knowledges-and-information-held-in-archives/.
54. https://www.nla.gov.au/using-library/Indigenous-cultural-and-intellectual-property.
55. 'These permissions pertain to the viewing of the Library material at the Library only. Further permissions will be required for copying, photographing or otherwise reproducing the material' (NLA advice, Cultural Authority – Permissions, provided by email June 2023).
56. Indigenous Archives Collective, 'The Indigenous Archives Collective Position Statement', p. 248.
57. https://www.nla.gov.au/using-library/Indigenous-cultural-and-intellectual-property, p. 12.
58. Kirsten Thorpe and Lauren Booker, 'Navigating Respectful Practice to Support Indigenous Cultural and Intellectual Property Rights in Australian Libraries', in Jessica Coates, Victoria Owen, and Susan Reilly (eds.), Navigating Copyright for Libraries: Purpose and Scope, De Gruyter Saur, Berlin, Boston, MA, 2022, p. 453. https://doi.org/10.1515/9783110732009-020.
59. Kirsten Thorpe, Shannon Faulkhead, and Lauren Booker, 'Transforming the Archive: Returning and Connecting Indigenous Repatriation Records', in Cressida Fforde, C. Timothy McKeown, and Honor Keeler (eds.), The Routledge Companion to Indigenous Repatriation: Return, Reconcile, Renew,

Routledge, Abingdon, 2020, p. 825; Genevieve Campbell, Jacinta Tipungwuti, Amanda Harris, and Matt Poll, 'Animating Cultural Heritage Knowledge through Songs: Museums, Archives, Consultation and Tiwi Music', in Amanda Harris, Linda Barwick, and Jakelin Troy (eds.), Music, Dance and the Archive, Sydney University Press, Sydney, 2022, pp. 55–77.
60. https://theconversation.com/rediscovered-the-aboriginal-names-for-ten-melbourne-suburbs-99139.
61. https://theconversation.com/after-140-years-researchers-have-rediscovered-an-important-aboriginal-ceremonial-ground-in-east-gippsland-155119.
62. Jason Gibson and Russell Mullet, 'The Last Jeraeil of Gippsland: Rediscovering an Aboriginal Ceremonial Site', Ethnohistory, vol. 67, no. 4, 2020, pp. 551–77. https://doi.org/10.1215/00141801-8579216.
63. Stan Grant and John Rudder, 'A New Wiradjuri Dictionary', Restoration House, O'Connor, ACT, 2010.
64. Jakob Wilhelm Günther, Grammar and Vocabulary of the Aboriginal Dialect Called the Wirradhuri, Appendix D. Charles Potter, Govt. Printer, Sydney, 1892.
65. As listed in https://www.anu.edu.au/linguistics/nash/aust/wira/.
66. Jakob Wilhelm Günther, Lecture on the Aborigines of Australia and Papers on Wirradhurrei Dialect, 1837–1840, Mitchell Library, Sydney, p. 162, FL661690 of B 505, available at https://archival.sl.nsw.gov.au/Details/archive/110367926.
67. Günther, 'Grammar and Vocabulary', p. 89.
68. https://aiatsis.gov.au/form/request-collection-access, accessed 04 December 2023.
69. https://collection.aiatsis.gov.au/austlang/about.
70. Legacy material can include recently recorded material.
71. Terri Janke and Company, First Peoples: A Roadmap for Enhancing Indigenous Engagement in Museums and Galleries, AMAGA, Canberra, 2018, p. 30, available at https://www.terrijanke.com.au/mga-Indigenous-roadmap.

ARTICLE
Anti-Racist Archival Description

Angela Schilling*

Lutheran Archives, Adelaide, Australia

Abstract

For those whose stories are in the archives, accessing them can prompt many emotions and reactions. People accessing these records, and those processing and providing access to them, may be affected by their contents.

There are many things we can do as archivists and archival institutions to make this process easier, more accessible, and safer for those who experience direct or intergenerational trauma. The profession has access to a growing selection of tools to guide our protocols and practices, such as the Tandanya Declaration, the ATSILIRN protocols and UNDRIP, as well as case studies for high-level institutional changes and cultural shifts, though this process is arguably only at the beginning of its collective journey. However, there are often immediate and practical ways in which we can implement anti-racist archival practice, including the way we describe archival materials.

This paper will discuss practical ways in which archivists can actively undertake anti-racist description work, and why it is imperative that this work becomes a priority in our collection management work. It will draw on the comprehensive document Anti-Racist Description Resources, authored by the Archives for Black Lives in Philadelphia's (A4BLiP) Anti-Racist Description Working Group, as well as other standards and sources.

Keywords: *Indigenous archives; Decolonial archives; Archival description; Autoethnography*

For many, accessing records can bring about a swathe of emotions and reactions, and our understanding of trauma in and around the archives is growing. People may be traumatised by the ways the records have been arranged and described, the process of physical access, and the information withheld from the records through redaction or other processes related to third-party privacy.[1] There are plenty of things we can do as archivists and archival institutions to make this process easier, more accessible, and safer for those who experience direct and intergenerational trauma – both users and those who work directly with records such as archivists or access workers. Our profession has access to a growing selection of tools to guide our protocols and practices – we are

---

*Correspondence: Angela Schilling
*This article is based on a talk first given at the Australian Council of Archivists Conference on Ngunnawal and Ngambri Country (Canberra), November 3, 2022.

slowly implementing the Tandanya Declaration (2019), the **ATSILIRN** protocols have existed in Australia since 1995, and the United Nations Declaration on the Rights of Indigenous Peoples (UNDRIP) continues to be a great tool for archivists in formulating protocols and policies. However, there are often immediate and practical ways in which we can implement anti-racist archival practice, including the way we describe archival materials.

I hope this paper serves to be a practical guide to ways in which archivists and other collections professionals can actively undertake anti-racist description work – work that can be done immediately but still with power – and why it is imperative that this becomes a priority in our collection management work. It will draw on the comprehensive document *Anti-Racist Description Resources*, authored by the Archives for Black Lives in Philadelphia's (A4BLiP) Anti-Racist Description Working Group, as well as other standards and sources. Although this resource was written in the United States, it is easily adaptable to our work here in Australia – anti-racism work can be conducted the world over.

The first half of the article will outline the idea of autoethnography and, for settlers who are doing this work, why we need to make the effort to truly acknowledge the trauma and emotion inherently within colonial and settler-created records.

The second half of the article will identify how archivists can use language, voice, style, and tone to describe records with anti-racism in mind – this section of the article can be used as a practical guide for archival description. Finally, the article will outline the importance of re-description in racist legacy descriptors, the care we need to take when using standards and classification, and the importance of transparency in description.

The use of autoethnography in archival practice

Adams, Ellis, and Jones stated that:

> Autoethnography is a research method that uses personal experience ('auto') to describe and interpret ('graphy') cultural texts, experiences, beliefs, and practices ('ethno'). Autoethnographers believe that personal experience is infused with political/cultural norms and expectations, and they engage in rigorous self-reflection – typically referred to as 'reflexivity' – in order to identify and interrogate the intersections between the self and social life.[2]

The way that this practice intersects with our work as archivists is to analyse our own personal and cultural experiences and use this as an active backdrop to our work. Archivists can use this standpoint as a beginning place in practising all parts of our professional lives; not only technical work such as appraisal, preservation, description, and access but flowing into post-custodial and immaterial work such as care for people whose spirits remain in the records, both living and passed; care for our colleagues, especially those from marginalised backgrounds; and care in thinking about the future of records as we look to communities for their guidance and collaboration in data sovereignty.

Jessica Tai speaks of the use of autoethnography in archival practice, when she states that in developing a liberatory descriptive standard, there must be an emphasis on self-reflection, and in surfacing the power that archivists hold through description.[3] When we reflect on our positionality and our own lived experience, we can begin to understand the positionality of others – of those within the materials, of the creators and of the caretakers. Simply put, we cannot conduct the decolonising and anti-racism work we need to do as archivists unless we have done this personal work, and truly work towards understanding how self-reflection and empathy fit into a theoretical and practical archival framework.

Autoethnography in the archival profession
The first aspect of autoethnography, or looking within our own stories to inform our values and the way we work, is to identify our cultural positionality, now and in the past, and how these inform our patterns of thoughts and cultural lens. While this may sound a simple task, it is important to note the lack of autoethnographic practices taught in tertiary information management courses, and the historical lack of introspection encouraged in professional settings, perhaps underpinned by a historical view of archives as a neutral space. While many professional settings may offer basic cultural competency courses as professional development, it could be argued that these often do not account for the diversity of professionals and their backgrounds, as well as targeting the direct link between our biases and our work.

Some questions we can ask of ourselves when thinking of our professional and personal biases are:

What is our cultural background and how do we identify?
Looking at our cultural background allows us not only to start to understand our own behaviours and biases, but also how we interact with those around us and the material that we work with. Understanding our cultural identities allows us to situate ourselves in proximity to others, to the ideas and behaviours we experience in other people, and in archival work, the creation of and content in archival material.

As an example of looking into our own stories to underwrite our current biases, I am the daughter of both European settlers and an Asian migrant, and I was raised in a middle-class, Christian, culturally Eurocentric and mostly English-speaking environment. I identify as Thai-Australian, a member of the queer community, as engaged politically yet not as deeply as I feel obliged to be. I feel aware of my cultural biases; however, I am also aware that my upbringing underwrites my behaviour without my consent at times, and that it is my responsibility to be aware of this when I am working.

Understanding the above factors allows me to begin to understand how I can relate to archival material that was created by other communities. I can ask myself how my own community relates to the creators of the records, and how my identity intersects with the ideas of the record creators.

What values were instilled into us as young people?
What were the values of those who taught us in formative years, whether they be parents and family, friends and their families, teachers or religious leaders? Why were these values held by these people? Did they explicitly or implicitly pass these values down to us? Were these values cemented by our environments? How do these values compare to the values we hold now?

How have our experiences shaped us?
Similar to how the values instilled in us as young people have affected our thinking as adults, our lived experiences shape how we view the world now. Are there any experiences in our lives that contributed to how we see other people, or how we move through the world? Have the places we have lived in or visited changed us? Have we experienced trauma in our lives, or have we witnessed others experiencing trauma? Do we have privileges that others do not?

What are our social and professional environments?
In our contemporary lives, what are the environments that we live and work in? Who do we look to for personal and professional advice, and what are the values and lived

experiences of those people or groups? Do we feel comfortable and at ease in our environments, or do we feel unsupported? Do we socialise or work with people different from ourselves? And how do we react to being in those environments and with those people or groups of people?

Have we undertaken any unlearning?
'Unlearning' has been very broadly defined as abandoning or giving up knowledge, ideas, or behaviours.[4] This process is linked to the notions listed earlier, of instilled values, lived experiences, and our environments. Unlearning can take time and persistence and is often uncomfortable. It could mean unlearning internalised racism, the way privilege informs thought patterns and behaviours, and many other values. Have we had the opportunity or reason to be introspective throughout our lives, either alone or with others, and has this introspection led to any unlearning?

While traditional ideas of professionalism and professional life revolve around the absence of personal values in a work environment, a post-custodial approach to both professionalism and practical archival work insists that we bring our personal experiences to the work that we do as archivists. Decolonisation work in the archives is inherently personal: memory workers need to do the work so that others, users of the archives, and our professional colleagues, do not experience further trauma when they access the archives. Furthermore, Michelle Caswell, in her work on feminist archival appraisal, calls on archivists who inhabit dominant identities to acknowledge their oppressor standpoints and actively work to dismantle them.[5] Without acting upon self-reflection and understandings of our own identities and biases, archivists risk inhabiting the same standpoints as those who created unsafe conditions within the archive that we are working to dismantle.

When we do this work we can come to acknowledge the real and visceral trauma that viewing records and reading descriptions can hold. Archival description is not just about technical description and metadata standards, but about creating an emotionally and culturally safe space to access records, and also a welcoming and appropriate physical space to access records. Anti-racist archival description lends itself to trauma-informed archival practice, a notion defined as a practice that provides a way for archivists to practically implement many ideas such as liberatory memory work, radical empathy, and participatory co-design.[6] Caswell defines radical empathy in archives as empathy that allows us to define archival interactions even when our own visceral affective responses are steeped in fear, disgust, or anger. Such empathy is radical if it is directed precisely at those we feel are least worthy, least deserving of it.[7]

For an archives user who enters an environment which they know can hold trauma, for that user to know that the archivist, the librarian, the access worker, or whoever is facilitating access acknowledges that trauma and understands their perspective, goes towards making that space safer. To acknowledge the fact that before we start any description that addresses anti-racism, we must fully acknowledge the trauma that can be inflicted by racist description, and we can then work to reduce the harm. To honestly and fully understand the intent behind our work is to provide the safest and most open anti-racist archival practice.

It is also important to understand the ongoing nature of autoethnographic work in archival practice. Just as self-development is a never-ending process, so is the practice of self-reflection within the paradigms of our archival and collective memory work.

Enlisting anti-racist description in day-to-day archival work
With the notions of autoethnography and radical empathy in hand as well as having access to anti-racist resources and communities of practice, it is up to the archivist and the institutions

they work for to apply them in their day-to-day work, or advocate for the resources to begin and train for the work.

Archival description and reparative metadata remediation is work that is tangible, practical, and can be applied to all formats within the archives. Some aspects of anti-racist description work, such as that of community collaboration and description co-design, are long-term and highly specialised decolonial work. While not all archivists will be able to implement immediate changes without discussion and differing levels of advocacy, much of this work does not require significant resources or significant shifts in policies or systems. Shifts in standards, protocols, and procedures will assist in cultural change and therefore easier access to this work, though often archivists can work within the frameworks they already have to advocate for and make changes to their thinking when it comes to descriptive practices. In this way, anti-racist description is a tool that archivists can enlist in their own efforts to 'decolonise the archive'. It can be a personal effort and while we can acknowledge that it is best underpinned by the notions outlined of autoethnography and radical empathy, anti-racist description can also be used to spark the shift in thinking about the way an archivist views material. In this way, the practical work can push the theoretical work, as much as the latter can push the former. Either practice can be an entry point into the work.

This second part of the article will identify some resources to help with beginning this work, as well as outlining some ways in which archival description and metadata can easily be created or amended to facilitate anti-racist work. This will lead to safer access to records for users and future archivists working on the records.

Anti-racist archival resources

Many practising archivists are often working in underfunded and understaffed community archives, with little time for research and professional development, and often no funds for access to national or international networking and learning opportunities. Community archives are just as likely as large institutions to hold material in need of metadata remediation, and often struggle with a history of outdated description, arrangement and appraisal practices, underpinned by the notion of the archive as 'historical truth' and 'neutrality'. While advocacy for professional development in the areas of data sovereignty, truth-telling in recordkeeping and archival spaces, and research into notions of 'decolonising the archive' are growing in the wider profession, practising archivists are often left feeling burnt out purely from their day-to-day work, leaving little to no energy for advocating within their own institutions. In these situations, communities of practice can be instrumental in providing support for those working with little to no resources. Communities of practice can not only exist as organised groups of professionals coming together to share stories and ideas, but can also extend to locally and informally sharing and using resources where possible, including within international and external communities that may be creating resources on similar issues and working within similar paradigms and methodologies.

One such resource, which has been instrumental in my own thinking about this topic and has also heavily informed the practical part of this article, is the document 'Anti-racist description resources', first created in 2019 by Archives for Black Lives in Philadelphia's Anti-Racist Description Working Group.

The document was put together over the span of 2 years, with an update a year after its initial publication. Its recommendations are intended to 'combat the racist structures inherent in predominantly white institutions, (which we also all work at) and in archival description of underrepresented and marginalized groups, in particular those in the Black community'.[8] While its immediate context and audience is situated in North America, the ideas and content are particularly relevant and appropriate in Australia. Indigenous records and those of other marginalised groups also suffer extensively from racist description practices, not only in the past but through ongoing practice which has not changed over many years.

The document includes the fact that 'metadata recommendations, an annotated bibliography, and an extensive bibliography, which aim to provide archivists with strategies and frameworks for creating anti-oppressive archival description, as well as for auditing repositories' existing description for anti-Black racism'.[9] The document is particularly accessible for practising archivists, is readily available as a free resource, and was not intended as an academic paper, making it a useful entry point into the work of anti-racist description.

Some easy ways to apply anti-racist description
Below are some simple ways to apply anti-racist description in a day-to-day archival setting.

Language
Considering the way we use language in archival description is an easy way to look at archival work through an anti-racist lens. A slight shift in language – the omission of a single word or the phrasing of a sentence – can have lasting effects on the meaning of the descriptor, and in turn on the access experience for a user.

There are many resources at hand which can guide us on safe and inclusive language. One such resource is the 2016 publication *A Progressive's Style Guide*, created by Sum of Us, a global anti-capitalism, grassroots movement of thinkers and activists. This is an accessible guide to inclusive language and while language is constantly evolving and shifting to encompass new spaces and communities, it is a great diving board to jump off from and start bringing meaning into the language we use to describe archives.

There are four central principles in this guide:

People-first language
The notion of 'people-first language' aims to make personhood the essential characteristic of every person. People-first language views other descriptive social identities that people may hold as secondary or non-essential. Instead of focussing on someone's race, sexuality, class, or other social descriptor, describing the person in the record as a *person* first and foremost will lower the risk of exploitation, judgement, or stereotyping.

Active voice
Also used in creative writing, the notion of using an active voice gives people in the records power and humanity, as well as agency and autonomy.

Self-identification
People who are robbed of opportunities to self-identify lose not just words that carry political power, but may also lose aspects of their culture, agency, and spirit. *A Progressive's Style Guide* is an excellent resource, and there are other guides created by and with communities who choose the language they use to identify themselves.

Proper nouns
Names used for and by individual places, persons, and organizations convey respect, understanding, acceptance, and clarity. They should always be capitalised.

In archival description, there is no need to use the language that is used in the material itself, if it is racist or problematic. While it is important to demonstrate and preserve the language used at the time, safer and more appropriate descriptions can be used for access purposes such as umbrella or heading titles. Original titles can be included in metadata with warnings or included on secondary or dropdown entries.

It is also necessary to think about the humanity of a person before describing their circumstances. For example, what is happening to a person, rather than being embedded in their identity? For instance, a person is not born as a homeless person, though they may be experiencing homelessness throughout their life.

Lastly, it is important to be aware of emotional and physical stereotypes, such as 'emotional woman' or 'angry Black man'. These stereotypes can be overt or subtle and are still used in social and media environments today.

Voice, style and tone

As we think about the specific words we use in archival description, we can also pair this with the voice, style, and tone of our descriptive writing. By thinking about language from a place of multiple knowledges and standpoints, archivists can take steps to unpack a western-centric mode of language and semiotics. Unlearning traditional descriptive practices is an essential step towards resisting the persistent inclination to value the 'neutral voice' within archival description.[10]

We can use an active voice when we describe oppressive relationships within archival material. The two statements listed further in the text, perhaps photographic captions, give an example of the shift in meaning by using an active voice:

Original caption:

Four Kent State University students were killed on May 4, 1970, during a clash between the Ohio National Guard and a crowd gathered to protest the Vietnam War.

Active voice caption:

Members of the Ohio National guard killed four Kent State University students during a mass protest against the Vietnam War.

As mentioned earlier, archivists can focus on the humanity of an individual before their identity when describing people. The example listed further in the text demonstrates using an active voice to demonstrate the humanity of the person being described:

Original descriptor:

…documents the business dealings of an Aboriginal Woman named Sally in Ceduna, 1927.

Active voice descriptor:

…documents the business dealings of Sally, an Aboriginal Woman in Ceduna, 1927.

While it is not always simple to change the name of a collection (though not impossible by any means), archivists should refrain from using flowery, valorising biographical notes for colonial collection creators. We can describe oppressed or marginalised people in records at least to the extent that you describe the creators. This gives the people in the records as much of a voice as the creator or collector of records and upends the power imbalance often inherent in collections named after colonial creators.

Use accurate and strong language such as lynching, rape, murder, genocide, massacre, hate mail, etc. Do not let your own discomfort censor the material; it is helpful for archivists to be uncomfortable with racist material, but not helpful to prioritise your discomfort above accurate description.

Archivists should describe relationships of power when they are important for understanding the context of the records. Often, these descriptions can be the only marker for the user to understand the complete context of the creation of the records or collection. Here, it is important for archivists to use their research skills to enhance the meaning and story, further than basic or traditional metadata might allow. An example might be when describing records created by figures who wielded power in multiple ways:

> 'Andrew Fisher was a known White Australia Policy supporter despite his legacies as Australian Prime Minister and worker's rights activist.'

Audience plurality

It is important to think about a plurality of audiences when writing descriptions, not only the audience who we generally see accessing the collections and finding aids. We might ask questions such as, are there any barriers to accessing this material and metadata for the communities whose stories are within the material? Is there archival jargon in the description or metadata? Is there clear, concise, and accessible wording? Is there academic language that can be removed or amended to be more accessible?

Who has connections to this material being described – are they being centred or even considered? Archivists need to consider the needs of those who seek to find a 'bigger picture' than just the content of the material – to rediscover their identities, understand intergenerational and community trauma, and to find coherence in their own lives.

Archivists can also consider ideas of alternate titles or provenance, acknowledging creators, contributors, and knowledge holders that are not named in collections, but have contributed nonetheless.

Community collaboration

Ideally, archival institutions will establish and maintain participatory relationships with communities to talk about description. This work of community collaboration differs from other reparative descriptive practice in that it demands more resources than most, and to be undertaken with great care, training, and planning. Those who are in leadership positions must acknowledge a responsibility to advocate for community collaboration with descriptive practices. A decolonial future of anti-racist description includes co-design of archival description with community members. Most western collecting institutions – government and state archives, religious archives, and private collections – need to build trust with community as part of this collaborative process. This is a long-term project, with the onus falling on collection leadership to allocate funding and resources towards these projects. While professional archivists have the skillset most suited to undertake collaborative description design and processes, community collaboration also needs a high level of cultural intelligence and training.

While there is much literature being written on this subject (to begin, see projects such as Traditional Knowledge labels and articles such as *Australian Indigenous knowledge and the archives: embracing multiple ways of knowing and keeping* by McKemmish, Faulkhead, Iacovino, and Thorpe, 2010[11]), it is the practical archivist's responsibility to begin thinking about paths for community collaboration, and how they could potentially feed into description projects. We can also take cues from those with longstanding relationships to the communities within the records and ask ourselves how to begin reaching out to communities through collaborators such as researchers, writers, current historians, linguists, and other community members.

Remediating legacy description

As mentioned earlier, many (if not most) archives are plagued with harmful descriptions created by previous archivists and librarians. Although an archivist may be aware that the descriptions are older and therefore using racist and other harmful descriptions, a user of the archive makes no distinction between new and legacy descriptions. These need to be amended with as much urgency as creating new anti-racist descriptions, and resources for this work advocated for with similar urgency.

It is always imperative to consider the audience when it comes to archival descriptions. Not only are people able to access records in person and through online catalogue records, but through third-party search engines, through an organisation's social media posts, and other methods. We should think about the harm caused by viewing descriptions, the connectedness of communities and shareability of archival records in a digital age, and sensitivity issues such as privacy, current political climate, reasons for incarceration etc. The users who may be affected are not simply those within the community, but those outside the community with similar traumas or experiences with power dynamics.

When amending racist descriptions or titles which are taken from the material itself, or provenance-led (e.g.: original folder titles), these can be kept as secondary descriptions, with notes or warnings. It is not necessary to keep titles for the primary reason of 'tradition' or practice that has never been changed or criticised. In addition, archivists can advocate for feedback mechanisms so that users and stakeholders can request amendments and additions to descriptions. This idea is underpinned by the notion of Right to Reply – outlined succinctly by the Indigenous Archives Collective.[12] Offering a space for feedback and reply supports ideas of participatory and collaborative frameworks, which in turn work parallel to ideas of anti-racist description.

Standards and classifications

Marisa Duarte and Miranda Belarde-Lewis describe descriptive standardisation as a 'violent process that inherently valorises some perspectives while simultaneously silencing others'.[13] Archival standards such as DACS, Library of Congress Subject Headings (LCSH), Dewey and other Name Authorities are all used to classify information in libraries and archives. This assumes that there are 'rights' and 'wrongs' in ways to identify groups of people and ways of knowing and insinuates binary ideas such as 'the other' or 'universalities'.

Anti-racist description looks beyond traditional descriptive standards and classification, drawing on the ideas of empathy and understanding of the complexity of communities. If descriptive standards are used in archival settings, consider the reasons why and perhaps, the reasons why it can or cannot be changed. If a harmful LCSH must be used, explain why that may be. While there are arguments for standardised language in archival description for accessibility reasons, free text should be used as much as possible, or standardised language can be shifted.

Furthermore, there are growing numbers of alternate descriptive standards that do not rely on harmful binaries and power dynamics. One example of this is the Indigenous subject, Languages and People thesauri *Pathways*, created by the Australian Institute of Aboriginal and Torres Strait Islander Studies (AIATSIS).[14] This standard is freely available online and presents a collaborative alternative to thesaurus created by Western institutions.

Archival transparency

It is important for archivists to think about gaps in the collections they are describing, and whose voices might be missing. While it is not always simple to fill these gaps through long-term right of reply projects, these gaps can be outlined in archival descriptions. If an archivist is describing material created by a collecting institution itself, they should be particularly aware of the gaps and attitudes towards legacy collections. These can still address these as legacy issues.

Part of an anti-racist description project is not only to acknowledge gaps in collections themselves, but to document the positionality of the archivist or institution, where possible. Finding Aids can include acknowledgements and notes such as who processed and described the collection, names of people who added to or made changes to the collection and descriptions, made decisions about the collection and description, and when and where these took place. This transparency not only holds archivists accountable for their work, but also acknowledges the positionality and biases that are inherent in description work.

Archival institutions can consider sharing an online statement regarding the language that they use in their descriptions, or description goals or policies. This is a good way to ensure those who are accessing the records understand why certain language is being used and assists in any questions they may have about the descriptive process. It may demystify the archival process for those who are strangers to the complexities of archival description, but it also solidifies the descriptive team's goals and can help with advocacy and sustainability in descriptive projects. One example of a publicly available language policy is shared by Melbourne University's Find and Connect project, found on their current 2024 website.[15]

Wider collection management policies can also be made available to the public, for similar reasons as discussed earlier.

Conclusion

Archival description is beginning to move from a static technical archival skill to one with an active, empathic, and collaborative framework. Anti-racist description can be used within this framework to bring about safe, inclusive, and reparatory archival access. The first step to an anti-racist archival framework is archivists using autoethnography to consider their own positionality in relation to the material they will be describing. When practicing archivists undertake this personal work, they can begin to understand how their descriptive work can bring new types of access for a wider range of users of the archive.

Part of anti-racist archival work is to acknowledge your own and others' discomfort when undertaking descriptive work, and questioning standard practice and policy, not allowing discomfort or fear to drive decisions. Archivists are encouraged to make their descriptive work community focused, not academia focused. Tools such as archival transparency, challenging traditional standards and classifications, and using voice, style, tone, and language to both amend harmful legacy descriptions and new descriptions are readily available to archivists without the need for heavy resources and significant changes in policy. It is up to each archivist to reflect on their practice, and how we can change the narrative for users – being staunch, open, reflective, active, and caring.

Notes on contributor

Angela Schilling (she/her) is a Thai-Australian archivist working on Kaurna Country. She was part of the 2019 International Council of Archives' New Professionals Program. Since graduating from RMIT in 2019, Angela has worked predominantly with Indigenous records and has a particular interest in Indigenous, migrant and vulnerable archives, and the ways in which archivists can work to mitigate ongoing trauma and colonial harm through practical archival work.

Acknowledgement

I would like to acknowledge the traditional owners of the land that I live and work on, the Kaurna people. I want to acknowledge the ongoing care and connection of the Traditional Owners of these lands, and that this care and connection is what allows us to live and work where we do – to enjoy the landscapes, to work in the archives, and to connect with each other. I also want to acknowledge the rich history and connection to recordkeeping and storytelling that the Kaurna people have always had, and that the western notion of keeping archives and archival structures is only one way – a colonial and often problematic way – of looking after and caring for stories.

The second acknowledgement I would like to make is that I am a non-Indigenous person of the land on which I am writing, and I come from a colonial-settler family. My mother is a migrant settler from Asia, while my father's family has been settled on this land for several generations. This makes me both a second-generation migrant child, as well as a descendant of a European migrant settler family.

Notes

1. K Wright and N Laurent, 'Safety, Collaboration, and Empowerment: Trauma-Informed Archival Practice', Archivaria, no. 91, 2021, pp. 38–73. doi: 10.7202/1078465ar.
2. TE Adams, C Ellis, and SH Jones, 'Autoethnography', in J Matthes, CS Davis and RF Potter (eds.), The International Encyclopedia of Communication Research Methods, Wiley-Blackwell, Hoboken, New Jersey, 2017, pp. 1–11.
3. J Tai, 'Cultural Humility as a Framework for Anti-Oppressive Archival Description', in E Arroyo-Ramírez, J Jones, S O'Neill and H Smith (eds.), Radical Empathy in Archival Practice, Special issue, Journal of Critical Library and Information Studies, vol. 3, no. 2, 2021. doi: 10.24242/jclis.v3i2.120.
4. CR Coombs, D Hislop, J Holland, et al., 'Chapter 2: Background', in Exploring Types of Individual Unlearning by Local Health-Care Managers: An Original Empirical Approach, NIHR Journals Library, Southampton, 2013 Jun. (Health Services and Delivery Research, No. 1.2.).
5. M Caswell, 'Dusting for Fingerprints: Introducing Feminist Standpoint Appraisal', in E Arroyo-Ramírez, J Jones, S O'Neill and H Smith (eds.), Radical Empathy in Archival Practice, Special issue, Journal of Critical Library and Information Studies, vol. 3, no. 2, 2021.
6. K Wright and N Laurent n 1.
7. M Caswell and M Cifor, 'From Human Rights to Feminist Ethics: Radical Empathy in the Archives', Archivaria vol. 81, 2016, pp. 23–43. https://archivaria.ca/index.php/archivaria/article/view/13557.
8. Archives for Black Lives in Philadelphia, Anti-Racist Description Resources, October 2019, https://archivesforblacklives.files.wordpress.com/2019/10/ardr_final.pdf.
9. Ibid.
10. J Tai, 'Cultural Humility as a Framework for Anti-Oppressive Archival Description', in E Arroyo-Ramírez, J Jones, S O'Neill and H Smith (eds.), Radical Empathy in Archival Practice, Special issue, Journal of Critical Library and Information Studies, vol. 3, no. 2, 2021.
11. S McKemmish, S Faulkhead, LM Iacovino and K Thorpe, 'Australian Indigenous Knowledge and the Archives: Embracing Multiple Ways of Knowing and Keeping', Archives & Manuscripts, vol. 38, no. 1, 2010, pp. 27–50.
12. Indigenous Archives Collective, Indigenous Archives Collective Statement on the Right of Reply to Indigenous Knowledges and Information held in Archives, 2021, https://indigenousarchives.net/2021/08/09/position-statement-on-the-right-of-reply-to-indigenous-knowledges-and-information-held-in-archives-released/.
13. ME Duarte and M Belarde-Lewis, 'Imagining: Creating Spaces for Indigenous Ontologies', Cataloging & Classification Quarterly, vol. 53, nos. 5–6, 2015, pp. 677–702.
14. AIATSIS Pathways, n.d., https://thesaurus.aiatsis.gov.au/.
15. Find and Connect, Language Policy: The Words We Use, 2018, https://www.findandconnect.gov.au/about/policies/language-policy-the-words-we-use/.

REFLECTION ARTICLE

Harnessing Social Media to Advocate for the University Archive

Laura Sizer*

Monash University Archives, Monash University, Melbourne, Australia

Abstract

In 2022 the Monash University Archives began using social media to advocate for and promote ourselves and our collections. This article reflects on the first 12 months of using social media, our experiences of setting up and maintaining our social media presence, the results we have seen and the lessons we have learnt. The key message conveyed in this article is that if our small team can harness social media to advocate for and promote our university archive, then any archive of any size can do the same.

Keywords: Archives; Outreach; Social media; access; advocacy; community; university archives; building relationships.

Background

Monash University (the University hereafter) was established in 1958 with the first cohort of students arriving in March 1961. The University began with just one campus in Clayton, but over the decades merged and amalgamated with a number of other institutions. These include the Victorian College of Pharmacy (est. 1881), Chisholm Institute of Technology (formerly Caulfield Institute of Technology, (est. 1922 as Caulfield Technical School), and State College of Victoria at Frankston, est. 1959), and Gippsland Institute of Advanced Education (est. 1968). Monash University is now the largest Australian university by student enrolment, has four Australian campuses, and a presence in five other countries including campuses in Indonesia and Malaysia.

The Monash University Archives (the Archives hereafter) was established in the early 1970s. We hold records of permanent value from across the University's Australian campuses, as well as the records of our amalgamation partners and predecessor institutions. We have 2.2 linear kilometres of records in our repository, including hardcopy paper files, along with audio-visual material, photographs, and a growing collection of born-digital and digitised material.

Despite our extensive collection, the majority of what we hold is not accessible or even visible to those who are not Archives staff. This is because we are still using a Microsoft Access database first developed in the 1990s as our archives management system. There are plans to

*Correspondence: Laura Sizer, Email: Laura.Sizer@monash.edu

obtain a new system in the near future, but until this happens we needed a way to facilitate access to our collections and to expand our reach and visibility, both within and outside the Monash community. This need was highlighted in 2021 when the University celebrated its sixtieth anniversary, where the Archives were only approached in a limited capacity to assist in the celebrations. It was becoming increasingly clear that few within the University, apart from those groups we had regular contact with, even knew we existed or how we could help them.

For our desired purpose of increasing our visibility and reach, showing off our collections, and advocating for ourselves within the University community, social media seemed like the perfect starting point. Therefore, in October 2021 we followed the advice of Strategic Marketing and Communications (SMC – later renamed University Marketing, Admissions and Communications [UMAC]) and wrote a social media communications strategy and created a content calendar with a year's worth of weekly content. Finally, in February 2022 we launched our Twitter, Instagram and Facebook channels, as well as a YouTube channel for our digitised audio-visual collection.

The majority of the work undertaken to plan, prepare, launch and maintain our new social media channels was done by one person in a team of four. This person spent approximately 2 weeks' worth of time on preparation, and dedicates approximately 1 h each week to posting content and monitoring our channels. Furthermore, this person and the rest of the Archives team have neither any background in media and communications nor any experience in communications or social media use on a corporate level.

Strategy

During our first 12 months of using social media we have learnt that being strategic is key to maximising audience growth and engagement. It is arguably quite easy to set up a social media account, post some photos from your collection, and return to business as usual tasks. This will achieve a goal of sending a message that your archive exists and that you have some interesting items in your collection, but it is unlikely to facilitate ongoing growth and engagement.

Planning

Our first step in being strategic was to plan. While we did not receive feedback on our communications strategy from SMC, the act of writing it gave us the opportunity to think about why we wanted to use social media, who our target audiences were, and what our intended messages were. Through writing our strategy, we established that our target audiences included staff, students (current and future), alumni, industry and media, and external individuals and groups. Furthermore, we settled on three key messages:

1. The Archives has a diverse collection of significant interest to the University community, the public and external researchers.
2. The Archives is a valuable resource on the University and its history, and the Archives team are available to assist with enquiries.
3. The Archives is a valuable repository for the deposit of records and other materials from those who are involved or have been involved with the University.

Once we had established our target audiences and our key messages we wrote our content calendar. This simply consisted of a Google Sheet outlining dates throughout the year, any applicable event on that day, the images we wanted to post, the text to go alongside those images, and a space to indicate which platform content was to be posted on and what stage it was at (e.g. drafted, scheduled, published). An extract of our 2022 content calendar can be seen in Figure 1.

8th August 2022	*Open Day over the weekend*	*Pick a photo for main post and then do some stories with throwback open day photos like how I did with o-week*	Twitter	Over the weekend thousands of people visited @MonashUni's campuses for our annual Open Day with an enormous range of activities, information sessions and displays. But we bet there wasn't a re-enactment of Ned Kelly's last stand by members of @MonashHistory like on Open Day 1981!	**Published**
		Monpix 2852	**Instagram**		**Published**
			Facebook		**Published**
16th August 2022	*Old student records focus*	*MON377 Caulfield exam registers dating back to 1933*	Twitter	Here at the Archives we have student records dating back to long before we started recording information in digital systems. For example, these exam results registers from Caulfield go all the way back to 1933! With results for courses in blacksmithing, shorthand, welding & more!	**Published**
			Instagram		**Published**
			Facebook		**Published**
24th August 2022	*45 years ago...Alexander Theatre*	*Monpix IN5226 - Alexander Theatre poster for 'Thunderbolt Rides Again'*	Twitter	Thunderbolt Rides Again! Performed at Alexander Theatre in August 1977. Described as a 'bushranging musical for children from 5 to 85'. One of hundreds of Alexander Theatre photos held in the Archives	**Published**
			Instagram		**Published**
			Facebook		**Published**
31st August 2022		*Gryphon 1948*	Twitter	Did you know that 100 years ago in 1922 what is now the Monash Caulfield campus opened as the Caulfield Technical School? After some name changes and amalgamations it joined Monash University in 1990 to become the Caulfield Campus. Take a look at the 1948 edition of Gryphon, the first edition of the school's annual student magazine, which features a lovely old ad for Repco. You can read all Gryphons on our website (link in bio)	**Published**

Figure 1. Screenshot of content calendar.

Evolving strategy

As the year went on, our strategy evolved according to actual versus desired performance. For our first year on social media, one of our main goals was to grow our audience and subsequently create visibility and awareness of the existence of the Archives. However, in July, our audience growth on Instagram had come to a standstill. After a quick Google search on how to increase followers on Instagram, it became clear that we needed to utilise more of Instagram's features, specifically Instagram Stories. We therefore began to post regular Instagram Stories throughout July and August, including throwback Open Day and Orientation Week photos coinciding with 2022 Open Day and semester two Orientation Week; throwback clubs and societies photos; and quizzes and polls about lost Monash buildings and what was on campus before it became Monash University. All these stories were shared by the accounts we tagged, including the official University Instagram and resulted in a growth of over 70 followers (78%) in those 2 months. We saw this experiment with Instagram Stories as a major success, and subsequently evolved our strategy and planning to include this feature going forward.

Collaboration

Using social media does not just have to be about your own channels, but rather the channels of other groups can also be harnessed to promote your archive. We have done this through collaborations with other divisions within the University, in particular UMAC who run the official University social media channels.

Our relationship with the UMAC social media team came about serendipitously. Once established, we created a content calendar similar to our own with weekly Archives content for UMAC to share on the official University social media channels. Much of this content was published to LinkedIn where we could not use it to our advantage or gain followers from it due to our lack of presence on the platform. Despite this, the content performed extremely well and proved to be UMAC's best performing social media content for 2022. Throughout the year, Archives content on the University's LinkedIn received 7,140 likes, 480 comments, and was reposted 150 times. The most successful of these had 1,252 reactions alone, 24 shares and 159 comments. We only began to see results for ourselves from our collaboration with UMAC in the form of audience growth in the latter half of 2022 when they started tagging us in content, thus sending their followers to our profile.

Results

Statistics

For the purpose of this article we are only going to focus on our results from Twitter and Instagram, as these are the two platforms where we actually engage with people. YouTube, on the other hand, has just been a platform for us to make our digitised audio-visual material accessible, while we created our Facebook account as a safety net when having trouble with Instagram as they are owned by the same company.

On Twitter, our tweets were seen 84,500 times, and we received 122 retweets and 948 likes. Our profile was visited 15,671 times and we gained 181 followers. This is on top of the following we already built during brief use of Twitter during World Digital Preservation Day in 2020. On Instagram we built our following to 240 followers, reached an average of 237 accounts with our posts per month, and had 791 post likes.

What content is the most successful?

Twitter

Determining which content has been most successful differs based on the metric used. Are the most successful tweets those that have the most impressions (have been seen the most times across Twitter)? Or are the most successful tweets those with the most likes? We consider both metrics to be as important as each other. In order for the tweet to be liked, it needs to be seen. Therefore, when first looking at what content is successful we look at impressions. This tells us which content is most likely to have the largest reach, which is generally as a result of the content being picked up by the official University Twitter and others for retweets. We then look at the amount of likes to see which posts are getting the most engagements (e.g. likes, comments, retweets) from the people who are seeing them. As Tables 1 and 2 show, the top 10 tweets do differ slightly depending on whether we are looking at impressions or likes. However, the tweets included in the top 10 are largely the same (with the exception of two), with only the order changing.

Tables 1 and 2 also show us that the most successful tweets during our first 12 months on social media are predominantly throwback photos. While these did make up the majority of our content for the year, we also posted a number of excerpts from publications, links to videos on our YouTube channel, links to Monash University posts of Archives content on LinkedIn, and current photos of items in our collection. Only two posts in the 'by impressions' table and three posts in the 'by likes' table are not throwback photos.

We believe there are a number of reasons why throwback photos dating from the 1960s to 1990s are the most successful. Firstly, there is a significant nostalgic element for people who may have been at the University, either as a student or staff member, during the time the photos depict. This is particularly the case on the Monash University LinkedIn where alumni and current and past staff are strongly concentrated and where these people tell their stories of their time at the University in the comments. In addition, these photos give a visual touchstone for current students and staff who can recognise a place and feel connected to the history of our institution. Secondly, the majority of these photos are black and white which visually contrasts with much of the modern content people will be seeing on their feeds. This means they may be more likely to stop scrolling, look at and engage with the content than with current colour photos of items in our collection, which may blend in with all the other content

Table 1. Top 10 tweets by impressions

Tweet	Content type	Impressions	Likes	Retweets
Aerial comparison of main campus	Throwback photo	4,441	45	8
Menzies Building LinkedIn post	Link	4,154	21	3
Forum now and then comparison	Throwback photo	3,524	29	4
International Dance Day	Throwback photo	2,829	19	5
International Day of Universal Access to Information	Current photo	2,702	37	9
Sir John Monash's birthday	Throwback photo	2,543	33	1
Monash Reporter Week 1 Semester 1	Publication	2,468	16	4
Graduations – fun outfit	Throwback photo	2,412	22	2
Dalai Lama visit	Throwback photo	2,331	23	1
Interim Council Minutes book	Current photo	2,110	7	1

Table 2. Top 10 tweets by likes

Tweet	Content type	Impressions	Likes	Retweets
Aerial comparison of main campus	Throwback photo	4,441	45	8
International Day of Universal Access to Information	Current photo	2,702	37	9
Sir John Monash's birthday	Throwback photo	2,543	33	1
Forum now and then comparison	Throwback photo	3,524	29	4
Dalai Lama visit	Throwback photo	2,331	23	1
Graduations – fun outfit	Throwback photo	2,412	22	2
Menzies Building LinkedIn post	Link	4,154	21	3
International Dance Day	Throwback photo	2,829	19	5
International Cat Day	Current photo	555	19	1
National Recycling Week	Throwback photo	1,910	18	0

on their feed. We are also not surprised that excerpts from publications do not perform so well, as they are largely text-based and significantly less visually appealing and engaging than photographs. We suspected this while putting together our content calendar for our first year, however it still felt important to share the Monash publications we hold which have online accessibility.

Instagram

On Instagram we focus primarily on the amount of likes a post receives to determine what content is most successful, as impressions for each post does not seem to differ much. Furthermore, it is difficult to compare posts across the year to determine which has been the most successful, because the number of likes on our posts has increased as our followers have increased. Unlike Twitter, posts on Instagram cannot be shared, except for on Instagram Stories, and content is only likely to extend beyond your audience if it is in the form of an Instagram Reel. However, on the most part, throwback photos generally receive the most likes on Instagram, just as they are the most successful type of content on Twitter.

Relationships

While the above information is interesting, it is not the only measure of success we have chosen to focus on. Along with audience growth and engagements, we have found that using social media strategically has allowed us to build relationships (aside from our relationship with UMAC) with other parts of the University, which we may not otherwise have had the opportunity to do.

One such relationship is with Monash Sport. On Instagram we posted an excerpt from a publication detailing the preparations for the opening of a new swimming pool in 1982. The post performed reasonably well for that point in time, but it also achieved two things. Firstly, we gained a follower out of Monash Sport because we tagged them in the post. Secondly, it encouraged Monash Sport to contact us via direct message to ask if they could have the photo used in the publication so they could use it for their own social media. Since this initial interaction, we have had a strong relationship with Monash Sport on social media. They like all our posts and have shared all Instagram Stories in which we have tagged them. They have almost 3,000 more followers than we do, so when they share our content, our reach is substantially increased.

Using social media has also given us the opportunity to develop the beginnings of a relationship with various University clubs and societies. More importantly, it has given us better oversight and understanding of the diverse range of student organisations that exist on campus and the activities they undertake. In late July and early August we began finding and following clubs and societies and various divisions of student unions on Instagram. Many followed us back, which increased our audience and our presence within the University community, particularly at the student level. Soon afterwards we created a set of Instagram Stories with throwback photos of student activities, tagging the clubs and societies that still exist and have a presence on Instagram. The Stories were shared by the tagged clubs and societies, who also subsequently followed us, and one group reached out to us about one of the photos used.

What comes next?

In 2023 we primarily want to continue growing our audiences across our platforms and continue to publish content that is exciting and engaging. To facilitate this, we put together a content calendar for 2023 at the end of 2022 based on the analytics on 2022's content. For example, we quickly learned in 2022 that photographs perform much better than snippets from publications, so we have ensured to limit the amount of content from publications in 2023. Additionally, we published polls on both Twitter and Instagram, which asked our audience what they wanted to see from us. These polls showed that our audiences are most interested in throwback photos and now and then photos. We have therefore ensured that old and nostalgic photos of the University are central to our social media campaigns. We have also included a monthly Now vs Then content stream where we try to recreate photos we have in our collection and post them as a side-by-side comparison to show how much the University has changed.

Moving beyond our first year on social media we are also continuing to foster our relationship and collaboration with UMAC, and we have already seen some exciting results from this in 2023. Thanks to the relationship we had developed during 2022, the social media team at UMAC asked if they could have a tour of the Archives. From this tour, they created a video for Instagram Reels which was viewed 10,000 times in its first 24 h, providing significant exposure for the Archives to the wider University community. This, as well as our success on Instagram Stories, has inspired us to explore making our own content for Instagram Reels in an attempt to get our content out to a larger audience.

Furthermore, our success on social media in 2022 has inspired us to explore other avenues for outreach and engagement in 2023 and beyond. For example, we are looking at how to utilise formal University internal and outgoing communications channels. We are also in the process of working with the Records Management team to take presentations out to faculties to talk about recordkeeping best practice, including communications about the Archives. Finally, we are wanting to offer more tours of the Archives and our collections, like the one given to the UMAC social media team, to more groups within the University. However, all these strategies are more resource and time intensive for a small team than using social media is. Therefore, social media will continue to be central to our communications and outreach activities.

The takeaway

Starting the journey of using social media to promote your archives and your collections can be intimidating. This is particularly true for small archives and small teams who may only see big state or national archives' use of social media as examples. But we have learnt that it does not have to be this way. Over 12 months of using social media, the team at the Monash University Archives have learnt that it can be a fun and exciting way to share our collections with the community when we currently do not have any other way to do so. The process does not have to be complicated and can take up as much or as little time as desired. Nobody in the

Monash University Archives team has experience in media and communications, but we have been willing and eager to learn and experiment. However, the key thing we have learnt is that being strategic is the most important factor in maximising audience growth and engagement.

Ultimately, the key message we have tried to demonstrate through this case study is that if our small team can harness social media to advocate for and promote our university archive, then any archive of any size can do the same.

REFLECTION ARTICLE

The Influence of Feminist Archival Theory on State Archival Exhibitions

Catherine Banks*

School of Art, Communication and English, University of Sydney, Sydney, Australia

Abstract

It has been widely noted in academic scholarship that over the last few years there has been a significant shift within the heritage and cultural sector towards more inclusive and community focused practices. In particular, the transition towards community accountability and institutional participation in social justice has meant that state archives are currently more open to adopting feminist archival approaches than ever before. Through the examination of two case studies within an Australian context, this reflection will explore the ways in which feminist thought has begun to influence the curation of archival data in exhibitions by state-run archives.

Keywords: *Feminist archival theory*; *Community archives*; *state archives*; *archival activism.*

Introduction

It has been widely noted in academic scholarship that over the last few years there has been a significant shift within the heritage and cultural sector towards more inclusive and community focused practices. In particular, the transition towards community accountability and institutional participation in social justice has meant that state archives are currently more open to adopting feminist archival practices than before. The relationship between community and state archives has always been inherently influential, as community archives themselves are a response to the limitations and failures of state archives. State archives are now in turn starting to respond to the observed successes and innovations of community archives. Through the following case studies, it will be argued that feminist archival theory has begun to influence the curation of exhibitions by state-run archives and bring to light feminist content with these institutions.

Developments in feminist archival approaches

One of the earliest developments in community archiving was the establishment of women-run feminist archives. Although women comprise half the population, their voices have largely been excluded from archival records. As such, women's groups have sought to counter

*Corresponding author: Catherine Banks Email: catherinebanks125@gmail.com

the historically male-dominated nature of archival institutions. As Rodney Carter has argued, 'Women, one of the groups who have been traditionally and consistently marginalised, have in recent history reacted against the patriarchy and the patriarchical nature of the logocentric archive, the "patriarchive"'.[1] As with many community archives, the very act of establishing an archive focused on women is itself an act of resistance against state archives which have sought to exclude them. However, the formation of women's archives in particular has been intrinsically linked to political movements. For example, both the Canadian Women's Movement Archives and the Australian Women's Archives Program were established in order to preserve documents of feminist women's movements which were in danger of being lost and forgotten.[2] In the case of the Canadian Women's Movement Archives, it was 'felt that the collection's credibility rested on the fact that it came out of the women's movement and was nurtured by feminists and operated in a manner consistent with those principles'.[3] This feminist archival approach seeks to recognise women's history which has been ignored but its intention extends further than that. Michelle Caswell and Marika Cifor conceptualised an 'archival approach based on the feminist ethics' as being 'guided by social justice concerns, that is, by attempts to use archival thinking and practice to enact a more just vision of society'.[4] By highlighting and preserving the history of women's political movements in the past, these archives legitimise women's continued political struggle in the present.

Importantly, however, in reference to feminist archives, Kate Eichhorn has argued that, 'What makes the archive a potential site of resistance is arguably not simply its mandate or its location but rather how it is deployed in the present' and so archival collections must 'be *activated* in the present and for the future'.[5] Therefore, the focus of this reflection is on the ways in which archives have 'activated' their feminist archival data through curating exhibitions. These exhibitions are inherently socially charged as they bring archival data out of the archives and into public discourse. In this section, a comparison will be made between two exhibitions which highlight feminist histories within Australian community and state archives.

'Putting skirts on the sacred benches' by the Australian Women's archives program

The first case study is the 'Putting Skirts on the Sacred Benches' exhibition by the Australian Women's Archives Program in 2006. According to their website, the Australian Women's Archives Program was 'created to build knowledge and recognition of the social, cultural, historical and economic contribution made by Australian women to public and private life'.[6] It was originally established in 1999 by the National Foundation for Australian Women in collaboration with the University of Melbourne as a response to concerns at the time about the fate of the personal papers and organisational documents of first wave feminists which were needing to be preserved.[7] Melbourne feminist Mary Owen, who had such archival material in her possession, 'galvanised the board to seek a sustainable solution to the mounting problem of what to do with Australian women's archival heritage'.[8] The foundation's solution was firstly, 'to establish a fund to support the preservation of papers', secondly, 'to convene a reference group of experts representing a broad range of interests to advise on papers that should be preserved', thirdly, 'to establish state-based committees that brought together historians, archivists, librarians and volunteers to advise the community outside established repositories and administer funded projects', and lastly, 'to establish a web-based register to publicise the location and content of women's material'.[9] Integral to this strategy is the concern not just with the preservation of women's archival material but also with ensuring the promotion and accessibility of this archival data to the public. Thus, 'activating' it as a tool of archival activism.

The two main functions of the Australian Women's Archives Program are firstly the Australian Women's Register, a searchable online archival database on Australian women and

Australian women's organisations, and secondly their online exhibitions.[10] The register is an example of a 'non-custodial' approach to archive curation as it is intended to 'link existing catalogues of women's papers in national, state and university libraries with the records of individuals and smaller, more marginal organisations often overlooked by major repositories'.[11] Unlike some community archives which resist any collaboration with state archives, this project seeks to bring state archival institutions and disparate community archives together in one place. The collections of both community and state archives are made more accessible as a result of the distribution of their archival metadata online. As Nikki Henningham and Helen Morgan have argued, the program 'as a digital, non-custodial model of curation, is designed to offer solutions relating to the dispersed and fragmentary nature of women's records'.[12] The project was always intended to be digital, and although there is now a growing trend of digitisation in the museum and heritage sector, at this time the digital space was still developing and not widely used by state archives. It has been a long-term characteristic of community archives to embrace the use of online digital formats, as a way of enabling public participation and enhancing community accessibility. Furthermore, as a digital format the register is not a static space, it is being continually updated and edited. It is a realisation of Stuart Hall's concept of the 'living archive' which he described as 'present, on-going, continuing, unfinished, open-ended'.[13]

This 'digital, non-custodian' approach is similarly apparent in the program's online exhibitions. They are an important part of the program's work not only for raising awareness about women's history but also for the opportunities they offer for external funding.[14] The reception of these online exhibitions has been highly successful and led funding bodies to see the value in publishing online in order to reach wider audiences.[15] As a result, the program has been awarded numerous grants by individuals, Commonwealth, State and Local governments, non-government organisations, and academic institutions to create thematic exhibitions on women's history.[16] As Henningham and Morgan have pointed out, 'Fifteen of the 20 exhibitions currently accessible via the Register were made possible by local committee fundraising'. One such exhibition is the 'Putting Skirts on the Sacred Benches' researched by Emma Grahame and Rachel Grahame which was funded in '2005–6 by the Sesquicentenary of Responsible Government Committee, an initiative of the New South Wales Government Premier's Department'.[17] The aim of this exhibition was to recognise the significant contributions and achievements of over 700 women who stood for New South Wales Parliament.[18] The political content and title of the exhibition are the clearest indicators of its activist agenda. Its title is a reference to a quote by Millicent Preston-Stanley in 1926, the first woman elected to the New South Wales Parliament, in which she stated, 'I'm not fool enough to suppose my going into the House is going to make any sweeping alteration. The heavens won't fall because a woman's skirts rustle on the sacred benches, so long the sacrosanct seats of the lords of creation'.[19] Although downplaying the extent of her impact in parliament, Preston-Stanley's words nevertheless draw attention to the fact that her mere presence in such a male-dominated sphere of power was a ground-breaking act and disrupted the established power structures of parliament. This sentiment underscores the ideology behind community archives, that the presence of groups in history where they have been ignored or silenced is itself powerful.

However, what is truly significant about the curation of this exhibition is the research methods that were used by the archivists. The exhibition's introduction acknowledges that,

> The challenges associated with research for this project were significant …. Many of the stories of unsuccessful candidates are no less interesting, but they are much harder to trace. Drawing upon a range of archival and web-based sources, the project team have managed

to track down over seven hundred names, and write biographical notes for over half that number.[20]

By using a non-custodial approach and researching a wider range of archival and non-archival sources the exhibition is able to uncover material and raise awareness about women's history which would have been easily overlooked in state archives. These resources include internet sources such as the Trove online database by the National Library of Australia and the online Australian Dictionary of Biography by the Australian National University as well as parliamentary scrapbooks from the New South Wales (NSW) Parliamentary Archives. By using a variety of historical resources, these women are put back into history and public memory where they were excluded before. However, it is apparent in this exhibition that there are ultimately limitations with the Australian Women's Archives Program which are common in community archives, namely a lack of funding and resources. Many of the 700 entries are very brief, some including only a name, political party, and the year they stood for election. Due to their status as a community archive, there is limited staff to research and compile entries and limited facilities to house physical material which narrows the scope they are able to achieve as an archive.

'Blaze: Working women, public leaders' by the state archives and records authority of New South Wales

The second case study is the 'Blaze: Working Women, Public Leaders' exhibition by the State Archives and Records Authority of New South Wales in 2018. It was originally held at the Whitlam Institute, Western Sydney University and is currently available as a touring exhibition from 2022 to 2025. The exhibition's catalogue has also been digitised online. In contrast to the Australian Women's Archives Program, the State Archives and Records Authority is the official archive for the state of New South Wales documenting 'the daily work of the NSW Government and its agencies from 1788 to today'.[21] The current iteration of the archives was established in 1998 by the State Records Act which renamed it the State Records Authority of New South Wales and defined its purview as 'to make provision for the creation, management and protection of the records of public offices of the State and to provide for public access to those records'.[22] It is prime example of the traditional purpose of state archives which was to preserve the juridical evidence of government agencies. The jurisdiction of their enabling legislation limits the perspective of its collection to those in state power. However, the influence of the 'archival turn' on their operations is apparent in their most recent 2022–2023 strategic plan. It claimed that their purpose is 'To ensure the people and government of NSW have ready access to archives and records that support good and accountable government, illuminate history and enrich the life of the people of NSW and their communities' and that their aim is 'to be a best practice regulator that is transparent in its operations and accountable to the people of NSW'.[23] In contrast, their 2017–2021 strategic plan did not have any focus on 'accountability', 'transparency' or 'public trust'. Instead, their purpose was to 'Preserve the records of the State of enduring value in perpetuity', reflecting the traditional role of archives.[24] We can see therefore, that there has been a recent shift over last few years within the state archive towards being a more community orientated institution with a greater sense of service to society.

This approach is seen in the 'Blaze: Working Women, Public Leaders' exhibition. The subject of the exhibition was an examination of over 150 years of a 'selection of women from the past who were trailblazers in carving out roles for females in the NSW public sphere'.[25] The similarity of the exhibition's theme to that of the Australian Women's Archives Program's is evident yet the latter was developed over 12 years earlier. The delay between exhibitions reflects the gradual influence that community archival theory is beginning to have on state archives. This change is made apparent in the exhibition curator Penny Stannard's acknowledgment that women's history has been omitted from official history and it is the role of archivists in state archival institutions to rectify this. According to the exhibition catalogue's foreword, 'Historical research within and beyond the State Archives Collection has uncovered stories of women whose achievements have, until now, been 'lost' to history. In other cases, new chapters have been written into the stories of well-known trailblazers'.[26] Although it is not an overt admission of the role state archives have played in this history being 'lost', it is still progress for a state archival institution.

The most significant element of this exhibition is its forward-looking activist agenda. As it claims in the foreword, 'Blaze aims to contribute towards current discussions concerning women in leadership roles and to generate a greater awareness of the trail that women in NSW's past blazed for those who followed. This unique exhibition melds past and present, and in doing so, enables greater clarity in the future thinking about women, the public sphere and leadership'.[27] There is a clear awareness in the exhibition of the effect that a lack of representation has had on women's lives in the past. This lack of representation has been conceptualised by feminist scholars as 'Symbolic Annihilation'. In 1978 Gaye Tuchman discussed the impact of symbolic annihilation in terms of media representation, specifically that 'They lead girls, in particular, to believe that their social horizons and alternatives are more limited than is actually the case'.[28] This is equally applicable to the representations of women in state archives and the public histories that are produced from them.

The exhibition openly addresses these issues. The questions that lie at the heart of the exhibition are 'What is known about the work of women in such leadership roles? And does a lack of knowledge and awareness about their work contribute to the underrepresentation of women as the statistics indicate?'.[29] These questions are strikingly similar to those posed by Caswell in her 'feminist standpoint appraisal' approach. Her suggested methodology for appraising archival material is to ask,

- 'Do these particular records under consideration give us the perspectives of those who are oppressed? Do they give the perspective of those groups who are even further marginalised within an oppressed community?
- Can these particular records be activated by oppressed communities for more robust representation, for efforts to achieve justice or reparation, or for inspiration to imagine different futures?
- What is the affective impact of my appraisal decision on oppressed communities?
- Who is left out of archives generally and the records collected by this institution or organisation more specifically? If we are to acquire this particular collection, who is left out? What is our position towards that omission?'[30]

The traditional attitude within the archival profession that archivists must remain 'neutral' and 'impassive' would have previously prevented such an activist driven discussion of archival data in a state archive exhibition. However, it is now becoming a more acceptable practice because the shift towards social justice in the archive sector has superseded the expectation to remain 'neutral'.

The extent, and ultimately the limitations, of the influence of feminist archival theory on the state archive is evident by the types of resources that were used in their exhibitions. A significant feature of this exhibition was its use of women's living testimonies, a common trend in community archives. Testimonies enable women to tell their and their female ancestors' experiences in their own voices. This is especially significant because women have been 'voiceless' in state archives for so long. By using their own words, the curator enables women to 'write their own stories' within the archive rather than speak for them.[31] As a result, women are able to exercise autonomy over their own representations while also lending authenticity to the state archive's narrative. This casual form of storytelling through personal memories and anecdotes reflects the more community and identity focused approach in recent archival scholarship which 'aims to recover and reassert the voices of record subjects in the archival process'.[32]

This influence, however, ultimately only reaches so far. Despite the claim that historical research for the exhibition was conducted from 'within and beyond' the state archives' collection, the resources referenced in the exhibition catalogue were mainly limited to material from the state archive's own collection and some collaboration with Australian universities and government departments. For this particular exhibition, the curator did not branch out to collaborate with any community archives and instead followed a custodial approach to their collection. This is not surprising as archival exhibitions such as these are often intended to showcase the archival data within their collections. In comparison to the Australian Women's Archives Program, the exhibition demonstrates that the state archive does have a much larger depth of archival material and resources at their disposal. The exhibition's catalogue is over 140 pages with dedicated sections on 35 women, and in-depth historical context provided throughout. While the Australian Women's Archives Program's digital exhibition included entries on over 700 different women, their entries go into much less depth. The state archives are able to use a variety of archival materials that the Australian Women's Archives Program simply do not have access to such as personal letters, newspaper articles, personal testimonies, and photographs from their collection. Their funding is also supported by the government, rather than relying on external funding. However, the curator herself highlights the absence of feminist archival records within their collection. Yet, the exhibition fails to interrogate the power structures that have led to this and the archive's own role in shaping the content of their collection. They do not take the opportunity to 'rethink both the process by which archival value is determined and the archivists' role in that process'.[33] Therefore, while this exhibition showcases the influence feminist archival theory and the 'archival turn' has had on the state archive's curation of their archival data, it still operates according to traditional archival principles.

Conclusion and the future of archive practice

As has been shown in the case studies above, there are strengths and weaknesses to both state and community archives. While community archives address many of the limitations of state archives by using more inclusive practices and focusing on marginalised groups, they often have a lack of resources and more limited collections than state institutions. There are often opportunities in state archives for a deeper perspective because of the larger scope of their collections and their access to more secure funding. As Caswell has argued, 'records created by people in power can serve the needs of oppressed communities, and in fact, are crucial for legal, cultural, and political efforts for justice and reparation'. Yet, as she points out, 'the explicit aim and orientation of feminist standpoint appraisal [is] to serve the needs of the oppressed rather than those from dominant groups, or, as in most appraisal epistemologies, to no one in particular'. This is why it is important for community and state archives to work together. There is a growing trend in archive scholarship towards increased cooperation between community and state archives. Cook described this concept in 2012 as 'community archiving' in which archives seek to be 'more democratic, inclusive, holistic archives, collectively, listening much more to citizens than the state, as well as respecting indigenous ways of knowing, evidence, and memory'.[34] This development is important because while community archives are valuable, it is also vital for state archives to evolve and incorporate broader perspectives into their archival approaches. From the case studies discussed, it is clear that state archives are starting to emulate feminist archival theory in their exhibition curation and that this has already begun to enrich the histories that they are able to produce. The future of archives is therefore for community and state archives to work together, which requires state archives to continue to evolve.

Notes

1. Rodney Carter, 'Of Things Said and Unsaid: Power, Archival Silences, and Power in Silence', Archivaria, vol. 61, 2006, p. 227.
2. "Canadian Women's Movement Archives (CWMA)." Archives and Special Collections of the University of Ottawa, available at https://biblio.uottawa.ca/atom/index.php/canadian-womens-movement-archives, accessed 20 December 2022.
3. Ibid.
4. Michelle Caswell and Marika Cifor, 'From Human Rights to Feminist Ethics: Radical Empathy in the Archives', Archivaria, vol. 81, no. 81, 2016, p. 42.
5. Kate Eichhorn, *The Archival Turn in Feminism: Outrage in Order*, Temple University Press, Philadelphia, PA, 2013, p. 160.
6. "Australian Women's Archives Program." The Australian Women's Register, 2020, available at http://www.womenaustralia.info/awap.html, accessed 13 December 2022.
7. Nikki Henningham and Helen Morgan, 'The Australian Women's Register and the Case of the Missing Apostrophe; or, How We Learnt to Stop Worrying and Love Librarians', The Australian Library Journal, vol. 65, no. 3, 2016, p. 167.
8. Ibid.
9. Nikki Henningham, Joanne Evans and Helen Morgan, 'The Australian Women's Archives Project: Creating and Co-Curating Community Feminist Archives in a Post-Custodial Age', Australian Feminist Studies, vol. 32, no. 91–92, 2017, p. 91.
10. "About the Australian Women's Register." The Australian Women's Register, available at https://www.womenaustralia.info/about.html, accessed 13 December 2022.
11. Henningham, p. 168.
12. Ibid., p. 169.
13. Stuart Hall, 'Constituting an Archive', Third Text, vol. 15, no. 54, 2001, p. 89.
14. Henningham, p. 170.
15. Ibid.
16. "Australian Women's Archives Program," The Australian Women's Register, 2020, available at http://www.womenaustralia.info/awap.html, accessed 13 December 2022.
17. "Putting Skirts on the Sacred Benches," Australian Women's Archives Project, 2006, available at http://www.womenaustralia.info/exhib/pssb/home.html, accessed 13 December 2022.
18. Ibid.
19. "Introduction." Australian Women's Archives Project, 2006, available at https://www.womenaustralia.info/exhib/pssb/intro.html, accessed 13 December 2022.
20. Ibid.
21. "State Archives Collection." Museums of History New South Wales, available at https://mhnsw.au/collections/state-archives-collection/, accessed 13 December 2022.
22. "State Records Act 1998." NSW Legislation, 31 December 2022, available at https://legislation.nsw.gov.au/view/html/inforce/current/act-1998-017, accessed 5 January 2023.
23. "State Archives and Record Authority of New South Wales Strategic Plan 2022-2023." State Archives and Record Authority of New South Wales, available at https://www.records.nsw.gov.au/sites/default/files/About/SARA22_Strategic_Plan_FA.pdf, accessed 20 December 2022.
24. "State Archives and Records NSW Strategic Plan Update." State Archives and Record Authority of New South Wales, 11 January 2017, available at https://futureproof.records.nsw.gov.au/wp-content/uploads/2017/01/RM-Forum-Ben-Geoffs-presentation-FINAL.pdf, Accessed 20 December 2022.
25. "Blaze: Working Women, Public Leaders". NSW State Archives, 2018, available at https://www.paperturn-view.com/?pid=MjU25662&v=2, accessed 13 December 2022.
26. Ibid.

27. Ibid.
28. Gaye Tuchman, 'The Symbolic Annihilation of Women by the Mass Media', in Gaye Tuchman, Arlene Kaplan, Daniels and James Benét (eds.), *Hearth and home: Images of women in the mass media*, Oxford University Press, New York, 1978, p. 53.
29. "Blaze: Working Women, Public Leaders."
30. Michelle Caswell, '"Dusting for Fingerprints: Introducing Feminist Standpoint Appraisal," in "Radical Empathy in Archival Practice," eds. Elvia Arroyo-Ramirez, Jasmine Jones, Shannon O'Neill, and Holly Smith', *Journal of Critical Library and Information Studies* 3, no. 2 (2021), p. 28.
31. Hall, p. 7.
32. Caswell and Cifor, p. 36.
33. Caswell, p. 6.
34. Cook, p. 115.

REFLECTION ARTICLE

School Archives and the Visibility of Heritage via #throwbackthursday

Julie Daly

Newington College, Sydney

Abstract

The purpose of this reflection piece is to discuss the visibility of heritage and the use of #throwbackthursday for school archivists and their collections. Social media is a valuable space for school archivists to share the wonders found in their archival collections. It is a way to connect with and provide positive engagement for the wider school community, providing connectivity, creating a collective memory and sharing intergenerational stories. In addition, this reflection piece provides first-person insight into how school archivists engage in #throwbackthursday, and why it is important to provide visibility for school archivists and their archival collections.

Keywords: *School archives; #throwbackthursday; Visibility of heritage; Storytelling; Personal narratives; Educational history; Social media*

Visibility of heritage for school archives is an enticing reason to enter the social media landscape.[1] Social media provides an accessible forum for archives to interact with the public and engage their interest for nostalgia and memory, and this interest can be utilised by school archives interacting via #throwbackthursday or #flashbackfriday.[2] Visibility for school archives provides access to a ready-made audience whose focus, whilst primarily centred around interacting with their school, can translate into a secondary interest in that school's history.

Archives are a valuable commodity, containing intrinsic information which uniquely identifies an organisation. For schools, archives contain a wealth of information with much of the collection photographic and perfectly suited to the image-based social media landscape. School archivists are the gatekeepers to their school's social, cultural and educational history who innately understand how to contextualise these photographs to underpin and promote visibility of this history.

Whilst each school's history is uniquely individual, the overarching core focus is the same: education. Within this crowded educational landscape, the question to be asked is: how do

*Corresponding author: Julie Daly, Email: jdaly1@newington.nsw.edu.au

schools position themselves to stand-out in such a crowded online space and shape the public's response to the school?

For most school archivists, there will be a regular request to contribute to their school's social media platforms. Whilst there are different and emergent ways for organisations to utilise social media as a 'fun learning tool', it is also a space perfectly positioned for engagement and connection.[3] As well as being a learning tool, social media can also promote in the 'shared act of collective memory' via #throwbackthursday.[4] If, as Steve Jobs once shared, 'the most powerful person in the world is the storyteller', then currently, the storyteller's power lies in the crafting of the perfect social media post.[5]

School archivists are using their storytelling platform to share images from the past to touch on collective memory and be framed within those well-crafted #throwbackthursday social connection posts. Whilst #throwbackthursday may appear overused or under-appreciated, most school archivists will use these labels to invite ease of access for informing and increasing visibility of their school's heritage. Such labels are an access point for eliciting 'fondness for a past event', where an individual bonds privately with a collective shared experience and find themselves part of a larger community in a shared space.[6] The truth is that 'schools are a constant in an ever-changing world', and archival images and #throwbackthursday social media posts can foster a strong and solid connection to the past.[7]

To interrogate the #throwbackthursday label is to attempt to understand why there is such a desire to connect so intimately with a shared past. For the school archivist, the appeal lies in communication of their school's history, and photographs enable easily accessible posts to be shared with an ever-growing and ever-changing community. For the social media user within that community, it provides an access point into an institution which plays a large part in their lives but whose history is often an unknown. Art historian Mar Gaitán posits that

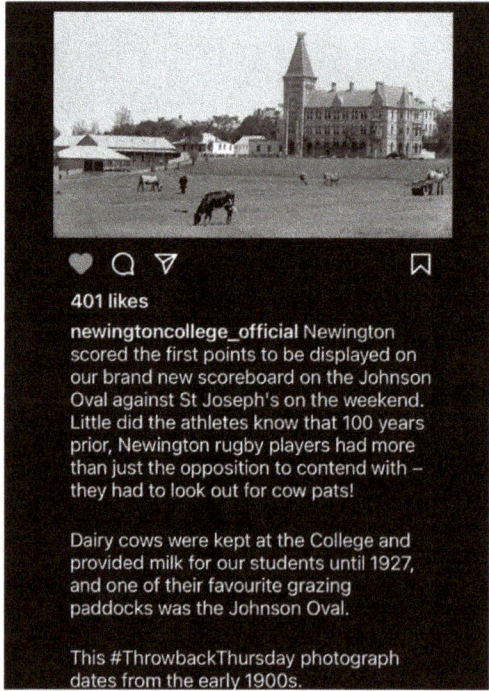

Figure 1. Newington College grounds early 1900s, screenshot, newingtoncollege_official instagram, Newington College archives.

social media not only allows the dissemination of history and memory but can also 'break the distance that may exist between the user and, in this case, the school'.[8] Just like that 'illusory barrier' of the fourth wall in theatre, social media – especially a feelgood archival post – can traverse with ease a perceived divide between schools and the wider community.[9]

The construct of social media should neither lessen the quality of the school's history nor the storytelling. #throwbackthursday is a vehicle for evoking nostalgia, promoting belonging, a collective identity and a sense of security that the school has both a long history and an archival collection, which is under the care of a professional archivist.[10] Whilst the theory underpins the value of social media, how do school archivists practice it in the everyday?

With the popularity of these #throwbackthursday posts, we can position our archives and our unique collections by harnessing memory and focussing on significant events, for instance, ANZAC Day, a commemorative day where people already possess a personal relationship with and express an 'intense historical connection'.[11] Such national days can legitimately position the archives front and centre in the social media of the school's official accounts, where school archivists can enhance the significance of our photographs and stories with an event, which already resonates with an audience. Historian Marianne Hirsch calls this resonance a 'sense of living connection', where access to intergenerational memory can attach to an event and translate into a sense of belonging within a community.[12] This connects current students with students past, presenting their history as relatable and providing connectivity and access to their own historical consciousness and institutional memory, not merely an exercise in nostalgia.[13]

Current events are another logical way to interact with the school community, creating a connection which strengthens a sense of longevity and importance as well as identification with the 'group collective identity'.[14] This melding between community memory and cultural history can work for a school, for example, where I used the occasion of a state election to share the narrative of a past student who had held that same high office being voted on. Another example of utilising current events for the school archivist was the death of a celebrity, a touch of fame via a school visit years past repositioned as a backdrop of connection with public grief. Such events might not be a logical link aligning with a particular school, yet these posts can attract alternative audiences interacting with our school's social media account. This creates a link in the chain of memory, which aids with 'group and community identity' and alters the perception of what might be part of a school's archival collection.[15]

School events are another access point for a #throwbackthursday post. These are school-specific events, perhaps a fair, sporting day or significant school birthday milestone. It is the perfect space to further embed that chain of memory and promote intergenerational engagement. One recent way I have used this was by celebrating a past student's milestone 100th birthday with a series of photographs for #throwbackthursday. Contextualising their lifelong engagement with the school, this social media post brought together generations and created an unexpected community joined in celebration, with multiple comments, re-posting and sharing which increased exposure.

For the school archivist, without the boundary of current or school events, the all-encompassing brief of #throwbackthursday can be quite a daunting prospect, as our archival collections overflow with opportunity and choice. These briefs may come from communications teams or alumni managers eager to exploit the cultural memory of the archives. How do I manage this all-encompassing brief? I tend to settle on images which capture the heart and soul of the school, or I focus on a recent donation to the archives, which highlights our collection and underscores the dynamism of school archives.

In my experience, there appear to be four major social media topic areas, which resonate with the community: positive profiles on incredible students, sporting achievements, anything featuring our youngest students and archival stories. All these topics enable the social media user to share in the school's achievements whilst also providing a glimpse into the past. Social

Figure 2. Stall assistants at the 1930 Newington College Great Wyvern Fete, screenshot, newingtoncollege_official instagram, Newington College archives.

media unexpectedly performs the function of recording our past, providing memory for those who have either forgotten or are newly engaging with a school's history.[16] This idea of social media as memory offers up images providing a connection to the past, as photographs, and therefore the social media posts themselves, become 'instruments for collective cultural memory'.[17] With this emerging era of artificial intelligence and deepfake images, it is comforting for the social media user to have confidence in the veracity of the images posted as the collective cultural memory sits inside the truth of a school archive.[18] The implications of this are, of course, much larger than school archives and our collections, but it does highlight how our school's images can play a part in underpinning memory and how we respond to it.[19]

Whilst #throwbackthursday does revolve around memory via the use of images, this social media landscape also provides a useful space to share potted histories of the school. Most school archivists are adept at writing longer articles for their various school magazines, which provide an access point for a deep dive into the school's history, perhaps via a feature profile or celebration of a building or school event. #throwbackthursday provides an entry point for a short history crafted around a particular image. I use this as an opportunity to share my knowledge, presenting interesting images alongside a précis of the history of the events. This underpins another role we as school archivists play, that of creating a narrative, educating and forming meaningful and positive engagement. #throwbackthursday offers access to official school memory, invites belonging to community, and provides positive social interaction and context for current events whilst enabling contact with the broader school community in an informal, yet official, setting. Social media users can comment, engage, re-post and share – at its core, these posts provide community and connection, which further embeds positive engagement with the school.

Is all engagement positive, or is there a downside to these feelgood #throwbackthursday posts? A school cannot always keep looking back. Whilst all schools have interesting histories,

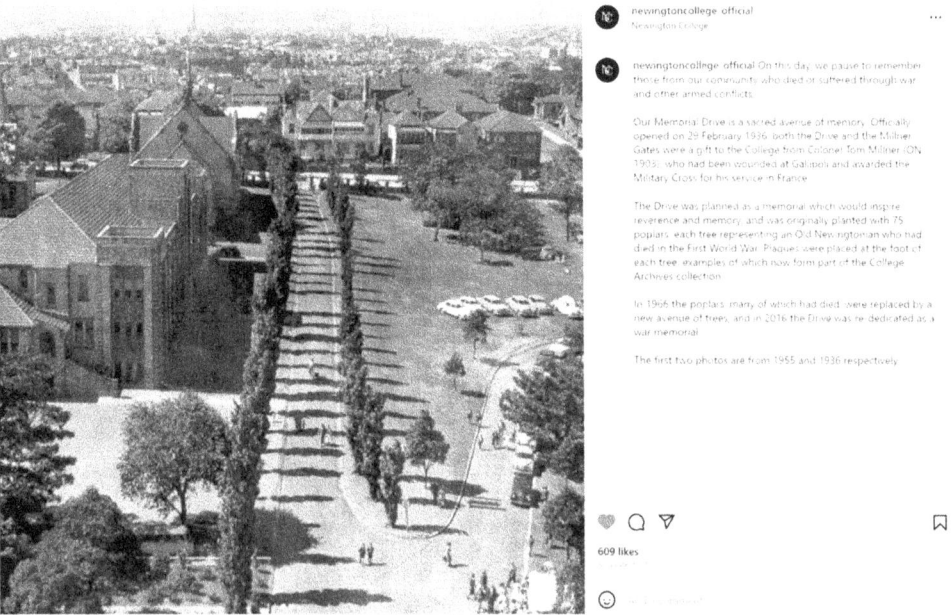

Figure 3. Newington College memorial drive, 1955, screenshot, newingtoncollege-official instagram posted on Remembrance Day 2022, Newington College archives.

ranging in age from recently opened schools to those that have passed their sesquicentenaries, schools need to show progress and show how they are looking forward whilst creating community and memories by looking back. Archival social media posts show this sense of progress through heightening a sense of belonging and providing connection to those who have left so they can continue their engagement with the school. Parents can feel a sense of community in a school, which can perhaps at times be isolating, and these positive good feelings carry into the future, perhaps through new enrolments, bequests, donations or just enhancing goodwill throughout the community. These are not the primary objectives of the role of the school archivist, yet we are, nonetheless, ambassadors for our schools and partly responsible for engendering goodwill whilst gently guiding the history of the school into the future.

Historian Anna Clark tells us that 'history shapes our consciousness', and social media enables us to shape that of our schools, whilst showcasing our collections, individuating us from our educational peers and embedding history and memory for the future.[20] Visibility of heritage is important for school archivists, as we hold a unique position where whilst our collections are not the school's core focus, we provide an easy path for connection. We should not fear befriending social media: writing our stories and fulfilling those requests for a #throwbackthursday post all adds to sharing the wonder found in our school archival collections.

Notes on contributor

Julie Daly is the college archivist at Newington College, a Uniting Church school in Sydney which was founded in 1863. Julie is a professional archivist who has worked in archives across corporate, non-profit, museum and educational sectors. She is enthusiastic about bringing history to life and is passionate about sharing stories from her collections. As a life-long learner, in 2022, she completed a Graduate Diploma in Local, Family and Applied History at the University of New England, which deepened her passion for social, cultural, educational and Australian history.

Notes

1. The school archives being discussed are those in Australian independent schools, which employ school archivists and run archival programs. All first-person accounts relate to my own experience after having worked in school archives for over 20 years.
2. For ease of reading, #throwbackthursday will be used throughout this reflection piece but refers equally to #flashbackfriday; Betsy Hearne, 'Leaving a Trail: Personal Papers and Public Archives', *Archivaria: The Journal of the Association of Canadian Archivists*, vol. 86, Fall 2018, p. 70, available at https://archivaria.ca/index.php/archivaria/article/view/13644/15045, accessed 4 October 2023.
3. Danielle Salomon, 'Moving on from Facebook: Using Instagram to Connect with Undergraduates and Engage in Teaching and Learning', *College and Research Libraries News*, vol. 74, no. 8, September 2013, p. 410, available at https://crln.acrl.org/index.php/crlnews/article/view/8991/9770, accessed 24 August 2023. For school archives, social media is a useful learning tool for sharing the school's history.
4. Mark Helmsing and Annie McMahon Whitlock, 'Time', *Counterpoints: Keywords in the Social Studies: Concepts and Conversations*, vol. 527, 2018, p. 38, available at https://www.jstor.org/stable/45178540, accessed 24 August 2023.
5. Dave Byrne, 'Steve Jobs' Lesson about Storytelling', 31 July 2020, available at https://www.linkedin.com/pulse/steve-jobs-lesson-storytelling-dave-byrne/, accessed 24 August 2023.
6. Helmsing and Whitlock, p. 38.
7. Melina Marchetta, Tell the Truth, Shame the Devil, Viking Australia, Melbourne, 2016, p. 283. This novel has as its central themes loss, tragedy and community, a community enhanced by collective grieving via social media.
8. Mar Gaitán, 'Cultural Heritage and Social Media', *E-dialogos: Annual Digital Journal on Research in Conservation and Cultural Heritage*, no. 4, December 2014, p. 41, available at https://www.researchgate.net/publication/340900068_Cultural_Heritage_and_Social_Media, accessed 28 September 2023.
9. Evan F. Risko, Daniel C. Richardson and Alan Kingstone, 'Breaking the Fourth Wall of Cognitive Science: Real-World Social Attention and the Dual Function of Gaze', *Current Directions in Psychological Science* vol. 25, no. 1, 2016, p. 70, available at http://www.jstor.org/stable/44318918, accessed 28 September 2023.
10. Veysel Apaydin, 'Introduction: Why Cultural Memory and Heritage?' in Veysel Apaydin (ed.), *Critical Perspectives on Cultural Memory and Heritage: Construction, Transformation and Destruction*, UCL Press, London, 2020, p. 1.
11. Anna Clark, 'The Place of Anzac in Australian Historical Consciousness', *Australian Historical Studies*, vol. 48, no. 1, 2017, p. 21. doi: 10.1080/1031461X.2016.1250790. While Anzac Day has a specific geographic reach and cultural context, the idea of any national or commemorative event can be imagined.
12. Marianne Hirsch, 'The Generation of Postmemory', *Poetics Today*, vol. 29, no. 1, Spring 2008, p. 111. doi: 10.1215/03335372-2007-019.
13. Clark, p. 23.
14. Apaydin, p. 3.
15. ibid., p. 4.
16. Roberta Bartoletti, 'Memory and Social Media: New Forms of Remembering and Forgetting', in B. Pirani (ed.), *Learning from Memory: Body, Memory and Technology in a Globalizing World*, Cambridge Scholars Publishing, Newcastle, UK, 2011, p. 85, available at https://www.researchgate.net/publication/259531789, accessed 29 September 2023.
17. David Bate, 'The Memory of Photography', *Photographies*, vol. 3, no. 2, September 2010, p. 245. doi: 10.1080/17540763.2010.499609.
18. Alan Trachtenberg, 'Through a Glass, Darkly: Photography and Cultural Memory,' *Social Research*, vol. 75, no. 1, 2008, p. 113, available at http://www.jstor.org/stable/40972054, accessed 4 October 2023.
19. Bartoletti, p. 91.
20. Timothy Michael Rowse, 'Distance, Dispassion and the Remaking of Australian History', *The Conversation*, 21 March 2022, available at https://theconversation.com/distance-dispassion-and-the-remaking-of-australian-history-177552, accessed 4 October 2023.

CORRECTION

N Thieberger, M Aird, C Bracknell, J Gibson, A Harris, M Langton, G Sculthorpe and J Simpson, 'The New Protectionism: Risk Aversion and Access to Indigenous Heritage Records', Archives & Manuscripts, vol. 51, no. 2, 2023, pp. 23–42. doi: 10.37683/asa.v51.10971.

The authors wish to correct a mistake in this article. The opening statement '[T]he task for linguists is to act as a channel to ensure that stolen knowledge and authority flow back to communities' is incorrectly attributed to Lesley Woods, but she actually cites it from Eira's[1] work. Later in the article a cross reference to that quote should similarly be attributed to Eira.

Notes

1. C Eira, 'Addressing the Ground of Language Endangerment', in M David, N Ostler and C Dealwis (eds.), Working Together for Endangered Languages: Research Challenges and Social Impacts – Proceedings of Foundation for Endangered Languages Conference XI, Kuala Lumpur, October 26–28, 2007, Foundation for Endangered Languages, pp. 82–90.

www.ingramcontent.com/pod-product-compliance
Lightning Source LLC
Chambersburg PA
CBHW080402030426
42334CB00024B/2967